MW00396410

Chi-mewinzha

Chi-mewinzha

Ojibwe Stories from Leech Lake

Dorothy Dora Whipple,
Mezinaashiikwe

Edited by Wendy Makoons Geniusz and Brendan Fairbanks

Illustrations by Annmarie Geniusz

University of Minnesota Press

Minneapolis

London

The University of Minnesota Press gratefully acknowledges the generous assistance provided for the publication of this book by the Leech Lake Band of Ojibwe and Mille Lacs Corporate Ventures.

Stories recorded by Errol Geniusz, Annmarie Geniusz, Mary Geniusz, and Wendy Makoons Geniusz.

The original audio recordings of Ojibwe Elder Dorothy Dora Whipple telling her stories have kindly been made available online and free of charge through the Ojibwe People's Dictionary. http://ojibwe.lib.umn.edu.

Copyright 2015 by Dora Whipple

All rights reserved. No part of this publication may be reproduced, stored in a retrieval system, or transmitted, in any form or by any means, electronic, mechanical, photocopying, recording, or otherwise, without the prior written permission of the publisher.

Published by the University of Minnesota Press
111 Third Avenue South, Suite 290
Minneapolis, MN 55401–2520
http://www.upress.umn.edu

Library of Congress Cataloging-in-Publication Data
Whipple, Dorothy Dora.
Chi-mewinzha: Ojibwe stories from Leech Lake / Dorothy Dora Whipple, Mezinaashiikwe; edited by Wendy Makoons Geniusz and Brendan Fairbanks; illustrations by Annmarie Geniusz.
Text in English and in Ojibwe.
ISBN 978-0-8166-9726-7 (pb)
1. Whipple, Dorothy Dora. 2. Ojibwa Indians—Folklore. 3. Ojibwa Indians—History. 4. Ojibwa Indians—Social life and customs. 5. Leech Lake Indian Reservation (Minn.)—Folklore. 6. Leech Lake Indian Reservation (Minn.)—Social life and customs. 7. Ojibwa language—Texts. I. Geniusz, Wendy Djinn, editor. II. Fairbanks, Brendan, editor. III. Title. IV. Title: Ojibwe stories from Leech Lake.
E99.C6W47 2015
398.2089'97333—dc23   2015006579

Printed in Canada on acid-free paper

The University of Minnesota is an equal-opportunity educator and employer.

21 20 19 18 17 16 15   9 8 7 6 5 4 3 2 1

Contents

Introduction:
Stories of a Leech Lake Elder

Wendy Makoons Geniusz

Dorothy Dora Whipple, Mezinaashiikwe, is one of the most amazing women I know. She is a grandmother, with five generations of descendants living all over the country, although she adds that most of her grandchildren live in Minnesota and Seattle, Washington. She is a fluent Ojibwe speaker who consciously held on to and continued to speak her language when many people of her generation were unable to do so. As she tells us in one of her stories, she remembers when one of her older sisters came home from residential boarding school unable to communicate with her siblings because she no longer spoke Ojibwe. Despite living in poverty and often having no assistance, Dorothy fed, clothed, raised, and loved many children. When I asked her what she wanted to include in this Introduction, she said, "I raised a lot of kids, mostly my grandkids." She had seven children, but she lost three, one boy and two girls. She formally adopted one of her grandchildren, and she was a foster mother for many years. She is ninety-four years old now, but I doubt that most people who meet her would know it. She is incredibly active, still living in her own home, and continues to care for her family, as she has for decades.

The Ojibwe People of Leech Lake

As she has expressed to us several times, Dorothy sees *Chi-mewinzha* (which means "long ago") as a collection of her stories, not a book about individual members of her family or about more general Ojibwe history. Some of her readers may not be familiar with Leech Lake history, however, so we will give a brief overview.

Leech Lake, like many present-day Minnesota Ojibwe communities, was a Dakota settlement during much of the fur trade. In 1763, a nearly sixty-year peace agreement between the Ojibwe and Dakota ended, and war broke out between these two nations. By the beginning of the nineteenth century, there was a firmly established Ojibwe community at Leech Lake. Anton Treuer states that by 1800 hostilities between the Dakota and Ojibwe had greatly decreased, and Ojibwe communities in Wisconsin and Minnesota were "fairly well accepted." Edmund Jefferson Danziger Jr. writes that there was an Ojibwe community at Leech Lake by 1780. Helen Hornbeck Tanner says that by 1810 the Ojibwe were well established at Leech Lake. Native historian William Warren, whose book (like Dorothy's) contains much oral history, writes in great detail about how the Ojibwe pushed the Dakota off their lands at Leech Lake, which he identifies as one of the last Dakota strongholds in the region. He credits Ojibwe victories in the region to more and more Ojibwe leaving Lake Superior and moving into the land that is now Minnesota. The Ojibwe reservation at Leech Lake was established in the nineteenth century, but its land base went through several changes during the late nineteenth and early twentieth centuries. Through the 1889 Nelson Act, which implemented the General Allotment Act of 1887 in Minnesota, the federal government parceled off portions of the reservation to individual tribal members and sold the remaining "surplus" land. This legislation resulted in Leech Lake members owning a mere four percent of their reservation by 1934. The establishment of the Chippewa National Forest in 1928 made it impossible for Leech Lake members to live on or otherwise use the resources of eighty-five percent of their reservation. Dorothy does not mention these specific pieces of history in her stories, but these events certainly affected her childhood in the 1920s and 1930s on the Leech Lake Reservation.

A Brief Biography of Dorothy Dora Whipple

Dorothy Dora Whipple, Mezinaashiikwe, is an Ojibwe elder from the Leech Lake Reservation in Minnesota. She is a respected member of the American Indian community in Minneapolis, where she has lived for several decades. According to her birth certificate, she was born on November 9, 1919, the eighth child of Gwayoonh, Charles Mitchell, from Leech Lake, and Ogizhiijiwanookwe, Emma Mitchell (née Earth), from Mille Lacs. Dorothy was raised with thirteen brothers and sisters in the Gwiiwizensiwi-zaaga'iganiing (Boy Lake) Community, also called Boy River, on the Leech Lake Reservation. Boy Lake is just east of the larger Leech Lake. As she tells us in her stories, most of her older siblings attended residential Indian boarding schools throughout much of her childhood. Maude Kegg, author of *Portage Lake: Memories of an Ojibwe Childhood*, was the oldest of Dorothy's father's children. Dorothy says her paternal grandfather, whom she mentions in her stories, was Sam Mitchell, and he came from Canada. Her paternal grandmother, whom she also mentions in her stories, was from Leech Lake, and she remembers her grandmother being called Chimaagid. Dorothy raised her children in Remer, Minnesota, near Leech Lake. She moved to Minneapolis in the 1970s.

Dorothy has worked on many Ojibwe language revitalization projects, and students all over the United States and Canada have learned from her language materials. I met Dorothy when we were working together on the University of Minnesota's Ojibwe CD-ROM Project. She and I spent three years making recordings and transcriptions for that project, producing five CDs. Language students love watching the videos Dorothy made for those CDs, including one in which she makes a series of baby swings in a grove of flowering crabapple trees while describing what she is doing entirely in Ojibwe.

Dorothy's mother, Ogizhiijiwanookwe,
Emma Mitchell.

Dorothy's father,
Gwayoonh, Charles
Mitchell.

Dorothy (right) *with her sisters Lucy* (left)
and Anna Mitchell.

Creating This Book

This book was Dorothy's idea, and she worked with us on every detail of it. In the fall of 2006, I asked her if there were any new language projects on which she wanted to work, and she answered me right away, saying that she wanted to write a book filled with her stories. She wanted this book to be illustrated because, noting her grandchildren's interest in comic books, she thought that pictures in her book would attract young people and inspire them to learn Ojibwe. She also thought the illustrations would help language learners understand what was being said, even if they could not understand all of the Ojibwe words. Some of the stories in this book were recorded prior to 2006, before I even knew we were writing a book, because Dorothy asked that I put every story I had ever recorded with her in this text. She also told me more stories between 2006 and 2009 that she wanted to include in this book.

We purposely did not annotate the stories in this text with historical or biographical information. These stories are wonderful examples of Ojibwe oral tradition because they are transcribed from the oral performance rather than having been written for this book. They are presented here as this speaker chooses to present them. Dorothy also had a final say in what went into this Introduction, and she chose to give only a brief introduction of herself, preferring to have her stories introduce her to readers.

It took a team of us to create this book. Errol Geniusz, Annmarie Geniusz, and Mary Geniusz all helped me make recordings of Dorothy at various times. Brendan Fairbanks and I transcribed these stories. Dorothy has certainly become a close friend, even a grandmother, of our team. When I asked her what she wanted to include in this Introduction, she said she wanted to say the following about me: "You're my best friend. You're more like my boss. You're a wonderful person who brings me food, wiisiniwin." We are all very honored that she chose us to work on this project with her.

Dorothy was able to help us transcribe some of the stories in this book, but she lost her hearing before we started preparing this manuscript. We were fortunate to find other Ojibwe speakers who spoke the same dialect as Dorothy to work with us on these transcriptions. We are grateful to all of them, and their names are listed in "Transcription Notes" at the end of this book.

We are very excited to have finished this project so that others may now get to know Dorothy through these stories. We hope that this text will help to revitalize Ojibwemowin and keep it with us for many generations in the future.

Miigwech,
Makoons

References

Danziger, Edmund Jefferson, Jr. *The Chippewas of Lake Superior.* Norman: University of Oklahoma Press, 1979.

Tanner, Helen Hornbeck, editor. *Atlas of Great Lakes Indian History.* Norman: University of Oklahoma Press, 1987.

Treuer, Anton. *Ojibwe in Minnesota.* The People of Minnesota. St. Paul: Minnesota Historical Society Press, 2010.

———. *The Assassination of Hole in the Day.* St. Paul: Minnesota Historical Society Press, 2011.

Warren, William W. *History of the Ojibway People.* Edited and annotated by Theresa Schenck. St. Paul: Minnesota Historical Society Press, 2009 [1885].

Editors' Remarks

Brendan Fairbanks

How to Use This Book

Transcriptions such as these have many uses. Educators might use these stories to teach their students about the Ojibwe way of life, Ojibwe belief systems, and Ojibwe cultural perspectives. For example, in a few of her stories, Dorothy talks about the sacred use of tobacco, its cultural significance, and its power. In another story, she talks about contemporary issues that she and other Native American peoples have had to face in today's society. On a lighter side, some stories are quite humorous. In one, she tells about the time some non-Indians painted themselves and dressed like Indians in order to harvest rice in the highly guarded ricing lakes. In another story, she talks about an older sister she and her siblings thought was named Shut Up because they did not understand her English exclamations of "shut up!" The stories in this book provide a glimpse of Dorothy's life, a life that only she can describe.

Given the language revitalization movement under way in Ojibwe country, these bilingual stories also serve as documentation and preservation. Embedded within Dorothy's stories are structures and discourse processes that exemplify the beauty and complexity of the Ojibwe language. The fact that it is a complex and challenging language can be attested by anyone who has endeavored to learn and study it. Many aspects of the Ojibwe language are still not understood well by linguists. Dorothy's stories provide linguists with more language examples on which to base new generalizations and research.

Teachers of the Ojibwe language may use this book in classrooms as part of their curriculum. They may give students listening assignments (if they have access to the audio files) to help improve the students' comprehension of the Ojibwe language. While students listen to these stories, they may read along to develop their reading capacity. Teachers may read the Ojibwe stories with their students in class to identify new grammatical patterns, words, or conjugational patterns. In more advanced classes, a focus on oral proficiency may be implemented in which stories are first analyzed for their grammatical and vocabulary content, then students could give oral presentations of the stories in Ojibwe. These are just a few of the many ways in which this book may be used.

Chi-mewinzha probably has its biggest value in providing the solitary language learner the ability to study the Ojibwe language. Not all language learners are able to attend classes, and a book like this allows people to teach themselves. I am frequently asked by language learners for "self-help" resources they could utilize outside the classroom. If this book is read while listening to Dorothy's oral performances, it becomes a viable self-help option.

I often see tattered language resources in the hands of language students, and I hope that *Chi-mewinzha* will also become one of those well-worn books familiar to learners in the pursuit of becoming fluent in the Ojibwe language.

Chi-mewinzha

Ogii-waabamaawaan
Chi-ozagaskwaajimen

Aanish niwii-tibaajim i'iw Gaa-zagaskwaajimekaag.
Mii widi wenjibaayaan idi Gaa-zagaskwaajimekaag.
Naaniibowa gaawiin ogikendanziinaawaa iw
baataniinowag imaa ozagaskwaajimeg, ge-sh
giiwenh gaa-izhiwebak jibwaa-dagoshinowaad
chi-mookomaanag imaa. Nimaamaanaan iko
niwiindamaagonaanig gaa-inakamigak iidog.

Aanish naa mii imaa gaa-taawaad anishinaabeg.
Jiigi-zaaga'igan gii-ayaawaad. Wenda-awibaa giiwenh.
Gaawiin nage gegoo aanakwad. Gii-waabamaawaad
giiwenh iniw Chi-ozagaskwaajimen. Ogijayi'ii imaa
gii-pi-mookiid imaa zaaga'iganiing. Gaye anishinaabeg
gii-waabamaawaad idi. "Chi-ozagaskwaajime,"
ikidowag. Mii-sa iw wenda-awibaa nage gegoo onji
aanakwad. Gaa-izhi-waabandamowaad giiwenh
enda-agaasaa aanakwad. Wenda-gizhiibide.
Obaazhizikaagon.

Azhigwa omaa naawayi'ii imaa, gii-ayaa ge aanakwad.
Miinawaa giiwenh chi-baa-baashkikwa'amowaad
idi, gii-nisaawaagwen iniw ozagaskwaajimen.
Mii gaa-izhi-gichi-awang gii-kimiwang. Mii
gii-ombinaawaad iniw ozagaskwaajimen.

They Saw a Big Leech

Well, I want to talk about Leech Lake. That's where I'm from, Leech Lake. Lots of people don't know that there are a lot of leeches in there, and also what happened before the white man came. Our mom would tell us about what happened.

Well, those Indians lived over there. They were by the lake. It was really calm. There were no clouds. They saw that Big Blood Sucker. It came out of the water, coming up off the water in the lake. The rest of the Indians saw it. "It's a big blood sucker," they said. There were people around the lake on a perfectly clear day, not a cloud in the sky. Then they saw a very small dark cloud coming from the north. It was coming very, very fast. It came right above the leech.

Then the cloud was there in the middle of the lake. And they [the thunderbirds] made lots of thunder, really loud thunderclaps. They killed the leech. Then it got really foggy and it rained. That's when the leech disappeared.

Gaawiin-sh wiikaa geyaabi ogii-waabamaasiwaawaan
iniw Chi-ozaagaskwaajimen. Mii i'iw
wenji-izhinikaadeg iidog iw Gaa-zagaskwaajimekaag.

Mii iw.

And so now they never see that Big Blood Sucker anymore. That's why Leech Lake is called that.

That's it.

Bagijigeyan Asemaa

Mii iidog miinawaa omaa ji-dazhimag a'aw asemaa.
Ongow animikiig bi-ayaawaad ayigwa, mii-sh giiwenh
asemaa, asemaa ji-asang. Mii-sh niin ezhichigeyaan
i'iw, asemaa aw asag agwajiing biinakamigaag aw
gaagiigidoyaan.

Mii giiwenh mewinzha iko iw gaa-izhi-noondamaan,
gaa-izhi-noondamaan gii-gichi-aya'aawiwag ingiw.
Ingii-pizindawaag niin ingiw chi-aya'aag. Ke-sh gaye
niin azhigwa chi-aya'aawiyaan.

Mii-sh iw wenji-dibaajimoyaan i'iw. Geget igo
indebweyendam i'iw gaa-ikidowaad. Ingii-pizindawaag
niin ingiw nichi-anishinaabemag. Biidwewidamowaad
ingiw manidoog, asemaa agwajiing ashi biinakamigaag.

When You Make a Tobacco Offering

I'm talking about the tobacco again. These thunderbirds, when they come along, we will put down tobacco. That's what I do. I go outside and put tobacco out where it's clean ground, and I talk with the tobacco.

That's what I heard from the elders a long time ago. I listened to my elders. Now I'm an elder.

And that's why I am going to talk about what I heard while they were talking. I truly believe what they said. And I listened to my elders. When you hear the thunder coming, go put tobacco outside on clean ground.

Mii giiwenh gii-noondawindwaa bimi-gaagiigidowaad
ingiw animikiig. Ina, ke gosha, mii omaa aw asemaa,
mii omaa apane aw asemaa bemi-ondinang. "Weweni,
weweni omaa bimi-ayaag! Gego, gego omaa, gego
nishwanaajichigekegon. Gidanishinaabeminaanig omaa
daawag. Mii imaa aw asemaa bimi-mikawangid."

Mii-sh giiwenh iko iw gaa-inaajimowaad ingiw
chi-aya'aag o'ow bemi-gichi-nishwanaajichigewaad
ingiw aaningodinong. Mii giiwenh iw dagwaagig,
oshki-aya'aansag ingiw, mii giiwenh ingiw
bemi-nishwanaajichigejig. Mii giiwenh omaa
gii-noondawindwaa bimi-gaagiigidowaad iniw
odabinoojiinyimiwaan ingiw, "weweni, weweni"
bimi-nanaginaawaad i'iw. "Gego, gego. Mii-sh
omaa endaawaad ingiw gidanishinaabeminaanig.
Weweni omaa bimi-ayaag.
Bimi-zhawenimig."

Mii-sh i'iw niin
wenji-izhichigeyaan i'iw,
asemaa asag.

8

They heard the thunderbirds talking as they passed by. You see, this is where they get the tobacco from. "Don't raise hell [which would cause tornadoes]. Our Indians live here. This is where we find the tobacco, where the Indians are."

The elders used to say that sometimes they go by and raise hell. That means they will have tornadoes. In the fall, the young ones are the ones who make tornadoes as they go by. They heard them talking to their young ones as they went by, "Take it easy," holding them back as they pass by. "Don't! Don't! This is where our Indians are living. Take it easy when you go by here. Pity them as you go by."

9

Mii-sh i'iw gaawiin gaye niin indabinoojiinyimag
gaawiin i'iw izhichigesiiwag. Nibiikaang igaye,
booziyan dibi-go nibiikaang, zaaga'iganiing asemaa
asig. Mii-sh i'iw ezhichigeyaan ayi'iing ingoji
izhaayaan. Dibi-go ge-izhaayaan, mii-sago aw asag aw
asemaa aw gaagiigidoyaan.

Miziwe gii-ayaawag ingiw gidanishinaabeminaanig.

Chi-mewinzha miziwe gii-ayaawag. Mii-ko
gaa-izhi-gaganoonigooyaan gaye niin i'iw, asemaa
ji-asag. Dibi-go ge-izhaayaan, mikwenimagwaa
ongow indanishinaabemag chi-mewinzha. Miziwe
gii-pimi-ayaawaad indinawemaaganag.

And that's why I do that, putting down tobacco. My kids don't do that either. And in the water, wherever you are getting in a boat, put tobacco in the water, in the lake. That's what I do when I go someplace. Any place I go, I put down tobacco, and I talk with the tobacco.

Our Indians were all over. A long time ago, they were all over. That's how they used to talk to me about it, that I should put down tobacco. Wherever I go, I think about the Indians long time ago. My relatives were all over.

Ziigwan, Niibin, Dagwaagin, Biboon

Miinawaa gegoo omaa ji-dazhindamaan.
Niwii-tazhindaan dash i'iw anishinaabe-ko
gaa-izhichigewaad ayigwa ziigwaninig, ayigwa
zaagibagaag igaye. Anooj gii-izhichigewag ayi'ii
ge wiigwaas gii-naadiwaad. Chi-bangii iko bijiinag
bakwang i'iw wiigwaas. Ingii-izhichigemin-ko pane.
Anooj gegoo gii-ozhitooyaang nooshkaachinaaganan
igaye. Mii akina gegoo bijiinag bakwang i'iw
ziigwang, azhigwa aabawaag ani-gizhaateg. Gaawiin
igo gabe-niibin gidaa-mamoosiin i'iw wiigwaas. Mii
gaa-izhichigewaad.

Mii miinawaa, miinawaa azhigwa giizhiging
i'iw gegoo miinawaa mawinzowaad. Mii-ko
apii nimaamaa, imbaabaa gaye, maajaawaad
azhigwa zaagibagaag babaa-naadiwaad mashkiki.
Onisidawinaanaawaan iniw aniibiishibagoon
waa-mamoowaad. Gaawiin dash ge niin gegoo
ingikendanziin, mashkiki gii-ozhitoowaad. Akina
gegoo ogii-gikendaanaawaa mewinzha anishinaabeg.
Gaawiin awiiya mashkikiiwininiwan gii-izhaasiiwag.
Gii-abinoojiinyiwiyaang, gaawiin wiikaa
ingii-izhaasiimin mashkikiiwinini.

Spring, Summer, Fall, Winter *(Version 1)*

I'm going to talk about something here. I want to talk about what Indians used to do in the spring, and when the leaves are coming out. They did all kinds of things, they used to go after birch bark. It's only for a little while that the birch bark can be peeled off. We used to do that a lot. We made all kinds of stuff out of birch bark, even that fan. Everything just peels, just after the spring when it starts to be sunny and hot, that's when it peels. You can't take that birch bark all summer because it won't peel, you can't get it off. That's what they used to do.

When all the berries are ripe, they pick berries. That's the time they go, my mom and my dad, when the leaves are coming out, they would go and search for medicine. They recognize the leaves they want to pick. I don't know anything about the medicine, the kind they used to make. Indians long time ago, they knew everything they wanted to use. Indians never went to a doctor. When we were kids, too, we never went to a doctor. They had their own medicine.

13

Miinawaa bagida'waawaad
ige. Miinawaa iniw ayi'iing
nibiikaang nimaamaa
ondinaad iniw ayi'iin
ozhitood ayi'iin apishimonan
ozhitood. Miinawaa
iniw, anooj-sago gegoo
ogii-ozhitoonaawaa, igaye
baasamowaad iw wiiyaas,
agwajiing baasamowaad,
mashkimodaang ayatoowaad.

Ayi'iing igaye iniw, anooj
gegoo miinan igaye, akina gegoo ogii-paasaanaawaa
na'inamowaad. Anooj ige gii-pabaa-izhi-goziwag
oodi-ko ge ingii-izhaamin, chi-waasa oodi keyaa
Zhaaganaashii-akiing, babaa-mawinzoyaang.
Babaa-mawinzowaad anishinaabeg. Mii iw keyaa
gaa-izhi-bami'idizowaad. Amanj igo minik oodi
gaa-ondendiwaangen, gaa-ondendiwaagwen,
babaa-mawinzoyaang. Adaawaagewaad iniw ayi'iin,
miinan. Chi-wawaasa izhaawag idi. Bimoondamowaad
ige iniw miinan, adaawaagewaad.

And they would go fishing with a net. And in the water, my mother would pull those rushes from the water to make rugs. They made everything and they would dry meat outside, and they would put it in a gunnysack after it's dry for the winter. Those are big sacks.

All kinds of stuff, like blueberries, they dry those too, all kinds of berries, they dry lots of stuff and put it away. They used to go all over and camp. We used to go far away toward Canada, picking berries. The Indians picked berries. That's the way they supported themselves. I don't know how long they were out there picking berries, a couple weeks maybe. They sold the berries. They walked a long ways in the hills. In Canada, they go in the hills to pick the berries. Two guys go hunt the berries in the hills. They mark where they found a lot of berries and that's where the people go. They're like scouts for the blueberries. They make a trail. There's always a buyer there, and a truck with all kinds of food. Then he buys berries. People came in the evening with boxes of crates of blueberries. There were a lot of campers there. They'd come and pack them up and sell those blueberries.

Mii miinawaa azhigwa bi-giiweyaang idash, mii
miinawaa omaa, ajina omaa bimi-ayaayaang
endaayaang, anokaadamowaad ogitigaaniwaan. Mii
miinawaa azhigwa goziyaang miinawaa goziwaad
anishinaabeg. Dibi-go keyaa izhaawaagwen
aaniindi-go onizhishininig manoomin. Mii miinawaa
idi o-manoominikewaad. Gabe-ayi'ii miinawaa idi,
gidasigewaad miinawaa bawa'amowaad, giizhitoowaad
iw manoomin. Mii-go idi endazhi-giizhitoowaad
i'iw. Gaawiin dash geyaabi izhichigesiiwag
i'iw. Odayaanaawaa iw ayaabajitoowaad.
Mii-ko gaa-izhichigewaad iw wiinawaa-go
ogii-kiizhiitoonaawaa, mimigoshkamowaad igaye.
Gii-gichi-anokiiwag ingiw. Gii-nitaa-anokiiwag ingiw
anishinaabeg.

Mii miinawaa azhigwa giiwewaad, o-na'inamowaad
i'iw ogitigaaniwaan. Mii miiinawaa azhigwa
bagida'waawaad giigoonyan, baasaawaad iniw
giigooyan. Anooj igo ogii-ozhi'aawaan. Mii-sh iw
miinawaa azhigwa bibooninig, mii akina niibowa gegoo
gii-na'inamowaad waa-miijiwaad gabe-biboon. Mii-sh
i'iw anooj gegoo gii-izhichigewag. Ogii-ozhi'aawaan
iniw odaagiman. Giiyosewag igaye, miinawaa
ayaawaawaad iniw waawaashkeshiwayaanan.

And then we all come home, we come home for a little while again and they work on their gardens. Then we move camp, and the Indians move camp again. They go wherever the good rice is. They go over there and rice. They parch the rice, knocking rice, and finish the rice. They finish the rice over there. They don't do that nowadays. Now they have their own machines that do that for them. A long time ago, they used to jig the rice and they'd parch their own rice. They don't do that anymore. They worked hard. They were good workers, they worked hard, the Indians.

When they're done here, they go home and put their gardens away. They go and fish, set nets, and they dry the fish. They fix them a lot of ways. In the winter, they put everything away and put all their food away for the winter. They do all of these things. They make their own snowshoes. They hunt and then they get the deer hides.

Ziigwan, Niibin, Dagwaagin, Biboon

Ayigwa ziigwan. Mii azhigwa zaagibagaag.
Miinawaa, mii iw apii anishinaabeg memoowaad
i'iw mashkiki miinawaa iw wiigwaas. Anooj gegoo
odaabajitoonaawaa wiigwaas, nooskaachinaaganan ige.

Anooj igo gegoo ingii-ozhitoomin.
Bineshiiwigamigoonsan igaye, miinawaa iniw
makakoonsan adaawaageyaang. Akina gegoo
ogii-aabajitoonaawaa iw wiigwaas. Apakwaanan ige
ogii-ozhitoonaawaa, ozhitoowaad iniw wiigiwaaman,
jiimaanensan igaye miinawaa wiigwaasi-jiimaanan.
Mii i'iw ayaabajitoowaad iw wiigwaas. Akina gegoo
anishinaabeg ogii-aabaajitoonaawaa iw wiigwaas.
Gaawiin dash geyaabi. Bangii eta-go izhichigewag.

Spring, Summer, Fall, Winter
(Version 2)

It's spring. Now the leaves are coming out. That's the time the Indians get the medicine and the birch bark. They use birch bark all kinds of ways, even for fans and baskets.

We made all kinds of stuff from the birch bark. We made birdhouses and little birch baskets and sold them. We made birdhouses and baskets. They use that birch bark all kinds of ways, for the tops of the wiigiwaam, little birch bark canoes, and the big birch bark canoes. That's what they use, birch bark. They use that birch bark all kinds of ways. But not anymore. Only a few people do that nowadays.

Mii-sh miinawaa giizhiikamowaad i'iw, mii
miinawaa azhigwa mawinzowaad. Akina gegoo
ogii-paasaanaawaa na'inamowaad editemagak.
Obaasaanaawaa miinawaa idi waasa-go izhaawag
babaa-mawinzowaad, zhooniyaakewaad
babaa-bami'idizowaad mawinzowaad iniw, miinan
iniw. Mii miinawaa bi-giiwewaad bi-anokaadamowaad
i'iw ogitigaaniwaa ajina miinawaa. Mii miinawaa
ezhi-maajaawaad idash, ingoji ba-izhi-goziwaad
babaa-daawaad jiigi-zaaga'igan, dibi-sago manoomin
ayaamagak. Miinawaa babaa-manoominikewaad.
Gii-pawa'amoog. Akina gegoo wiinawaa
ogii-ozhitoonaawaa. Wiinawaa-go ogii-kiizhitoonaawaa
iw manoomin, gii-kidasamowaad igaye. Mii miinawaa
nooshkaachigewaad mii iniw gaa-aabajitoowaad iniw
nooshkaachinaaganan, mii imaa iw wiigwaas imaa
gii-ozhitoowaad, miinawaa gii-mimigoshkamowaad.
Ogii-ozhitoonaawaa gaye iw imaa dash
mimigoshkamowaad. Bashkwegino-makizinan ige
baazikamowaajin. Gaawiin ige obookoshkanziinaawaa
iw, iw manoomin mimigoshkamowaad. Gii-onizhishin
i'iw gii-izhichigewaad.

Mii-sh imaa kawe iw, gegoo-go wii-izhichigewaad iko
gii-mawinzowaad miinawaa manoominikewaad, akawe
zagaswe'idiwag. Wiisiniwin odatoonaawaa miinawaa
asemaan.

When they finish, they pick berries. They dry the berries and put them away. They dry them and go far away to pick berries, and made money to support themselves picking berries, blueberries. They come home and go work on their garden a little. They leave again and go camp someplace else close to the lake or river, wherever there's rice. They go around ricing. They went out and riced. They made everything. They finish their own rice, and they parched it. They fan the rice. That's what they use as a fan, birch bark baskets. They use that birch bark, and they jig the rice. They made a place to jig the rice. They have to wear moccasins. They don't break the rice when they jig the rice. That was a good way to do it.

When they got the berries and the rice, they first have a feast. They put out some food and tobacco. They first have a feast for the rice they want to eat, and for the blueberries, when they want to eat them for the first time. That's what they used to do, putting out tobacco.

Akawe da-zagaswe'idiwag waa-miijiwaad i'iw
manoomin miinawaa iniw miinan oshki-miijiwaad. Mii
gaa-izhichigewaad iko, asemaan asaawaad.

Ke i'iw, manoomin i'iw wayeshkad
ezhi-bawa'amowaad. Mii-sh iw giizhitoowaad iw
manoomin. Mii-sh igo imaa ashangewaad imaa,
asemaan ge imaa asaawaad. Nandomaawaad iniw
aanind anishinaaben akina oshki-miijiwaad iw
manoomin. Mii gaa-izhichigewaad aw anishinaabeg.
Weweni gii-izhichigewag.

Mii-sh i'iw weweni dash i'iw gii-miinindwaa
iw manoomin weweni, gego ge
ji-bimi-nishwanaajichigesigwaa ingiw animikiig
ji-bimi-mamoowaad i'iw, giishpin gwayakochigesigwaa
ingiw anishinaabeg. Gaawiin dash geyaabi iw
ingikendanziin awiiya ji-izhichiged. Mii miinawaa
azhigwa ishkwaa-manoominikewaad miinawaa
giiwewaad endaawaad, mii miinawaa bagida'waawaad
agoonaawaad iniw giigoonyan agwajiing
mashkawaakwajimaawaad.

Gaawiin igaye ingiw asaawensag, gaawiin awiiya
ogii-pabaamenimaasiwaawaan iniw giigoonyan.
Ogii-abwenaawaan ige iniw iniw giigoonyan.
Miinawaa gii-wanii'igewag, miinawaa giiyosewaad.
Weweni gii-pami'idizowag. Gii-gichi-anokiiwag ingiw
anishinaabeg. Gaawiin ige awiiya gii-aakozisiin.

They go after the rice, they finish the rice, and then they have a feast. They feed, and put out tobacco. The other Indians are invited to come eat the first part of the rice. That's what the Indians used to do. They did it right.

And that's the reason why the Indians got rice, because they put out tobacco for the thunder not to come to destroy the rice. They will come and take the rice if the Indians don't do it right. I don't know anybody that does that anymore. When they finish ricing, they go home, and then they set net again, and hang their fish outside and freeze them.

No one bothered the fish. They also cooked the fish. And then they trap and hunt. They took care of themselves. The Indians worked hard. Nobody was sick.

Ke dash noongom, mii-sa eta-go apane aakoziwaad
ingiw anishinaabeg. Gii-onizhishinini gaa-miijiwaad.
Ke-sh noongom anooj inaapinem, apane nibowaad
ingiw anishinaabeg. Mewinzha-sh gaawiin
gii-izhiwebasinoon i'iw. Gaawiin ige awiiya
mashkikiiwininiwan ogii-aabaji'aawaasiwaawaan.
Wiinawaa-go mashkiki ogii-ozhitoonaawaa. Mii-sh
noongom, gidinigaa'igoomin anishinaabewiyang.

Mii iw eta go ekidoyaan.

Nowadays, the Indians are always sick. They ate good food. But see nowadays, there's a lot of sickness, and a lot of the Indians are dying. See nowadays, a lot of Indians are sick. But a long time ago, it wasn't like that. They didn't use doctors a long time ago. They make their own medicine. Nowadays they abuse the Indians.

That's all I'm saying.

Iskigamizigeng

Mii omaa gagwejimigooyaan omaa ji-dazhindamaan
i'iw iskigamizigan. Ingii-iskigamizige iko gaye niin.

Nimaamaa gaye gii-iskigamizige. Gaye niinawind
igo ingii-iskigamizigemin iko. Mii a'aw omaa iidog
dadazhindamaan i'iw babaa-ozhiga'iged a'aw,
ozhiga'iged. Mii ezhichigeyaan.

Bakaan dash omaa chi-mookomaanag keyaa
izhichigewag.

Ayi'ii-ko gii-ozhiga'igewaad, waagaakwad i'iw
gaa-aabajitoowaad. Miinawaa ogii-ozhitoonaawaa iniw
ayi'iin anishinaabeg gaa-izhichigewaad. Bebakaan dash
izhichigewag noongom.

Ayi'iin ge wiigwaasi-makakoon iniw
gaa-aabajitoowaajin gii-iskigamizigewaad.
Eni-babaa-naadoobiiwaad gigizheb, maawanjitoowaad
i'iw nibi. Miinawaa ayi'iin iniw akikoon iniw
gaa-aabaji'aajin, *okaadakikoon* gii-izhinikaazowag
ingiw akikoog iko nimaamaaa gaa-ayaawaajin.
Gaawiin ge wiikaa niwaabamaasiig ingiw. Bakaan-sa
bi-izhichigewag noongom.

Boiling Sap

They've asked me to talk about
sugar bush. I used to boil
sap too. My mom too used to
boil sap. We used to boil sap
sometimes. What I'm talking
about here is [my mom] going
around tapping trees. That's
what I'm doing now.

The white people here do it a
different way. When they tapped
the trees, they used an axe. The
Indians made everything [like
taps] is what the Indians did.
Everyone does it differently
nowadays.

They used to use these birch
bark boxes when they were sugaring. They collect
the sap in the morning, and they collect the water.
These pails they used, they are called *okaadakikoon*
[a kettle with legs], the pails my mother used to have.
I don't see them anymore. Anyways, things are done
differently now.

Gii-ozhiga'igewaad, maawanjitoowaad
iskigamizigewaad, iskigamizigeng. Ayi'iing dash
omaa, mazinaakide omaa, babaa-naadoobiiwaad
igaye. Baa-naadoobiiyaang iko gigizheb. Gaawiin ige,
gimiwaninig igaye, ezhi-ziigwebinamaang. Gaawiin
i'iw gidaa-aabajitoosiin i'iw nibi imaa gii-kimiwang.
Ezhi-ziigwebinigaadeg i'iw. Meta-go iw ayi'ii, mitigoon
eta-go.

Mii-sh miinawaa azhigwa onzamowaad i'iw,
onzamowaad i'iw, ingwana i'iw, ayi'iin dash idi omaa
niwaabanda'igoo omaa, aw giizhikaandag imaa,
ayaawaawaad iniw gizhikaandagoon aabaji'aawaad.
Ayi'iin iniw iidog gaa-onji-aabaji'aad iniw
giizhikaandag i'iw ji-ziigigamideg i'iw ziinzibaakwad
ziinzibaakwadoons. Meta maa aabaji'aawaad iniw
giizhikaandagoon—ziigigamideg i'iw ziinzibaakwad.

Mii-sh miinawaa i'iw, ayigwa aabita azhigwa
giizizamowaad, gaawiin geyaabi odaabaji'aasiwaawaan
iniw. Ayi'ii dash i'iw, abwiins i'iw ogii-ozhitoonaawaan
mitig. Mii i'iw oninawe'amowaad i'iw ziinzibaakwad.
Gaa-izhi-gikendamowaad iw minik waa-kiizizamowaad,
zhiiwaagamizigan ozhitoowaad. Maagizhaa ge
iniw ziiga'igaansan ige ozhitoowaad miinawaa iw
ziinzibaakwad.

Ayi'ii iko imaa gaa-apagidoowaad nimaamaa atooyaang
ayi'ii doodooshaaboo-bimide, giizizamaang i'iw
ziinzibaakwad,

28

They tapped the trees, put all the sap into one kettle, and it's boiled. And this here in this picture, they are also going around collecting sap. We used to go around collecting sap early in the morning. When it rained, we'd go dump it out. You shouldn't use the water in there when it rained. And so it was dumped out. Only the sticks.

And when they are boiling it, and here they are showing me cedar boughs, having cedar boughs and using them. The reason they are using those cedar boughs is if the sap should boil over. Only then do they use the cedar boughs—when the sugar is boiling over.

When it is half done, they don't use them anymore. They made a little wooden paddle out of a stick. Then they stir the sugar. They knew how much they wanted to cook it down when they made syrup. Or when they made those little sugar cakes and maple sugar.

Mii-sh i'iw ayi'ii, ziinzibaakwad i'iw ozhitooyaang.

Odoozhitoonaawaa iw mitigo-makakoons i'iw,
giizhitoowaad i'iw ziinzibaakwad naa ziiga'igaansan,
zhiiwaagamizigan.

Gaa-izhi-gikendamaang apii minik, ayi'ii aw goon
ayaabaji'angid waa-apiichigamideg i'iw ziinzibaakwad.
Mii gaa-aabaji'angid a'aw goon giizhideg i'iw. Gaawiin
ge gidaa-jaagizanziin i'iw. Gaawiin gidaa-jaagizanziin.
Ezhi-gikendamaang i'iw minik gaa-kiizizamaan i'iw
wii-ozhitooyang gegoo.

Chi-anokiiwin igo iw. Gaawiin geyaabi gwech
awiiya. Chi-mookomaanag, ingiw idash gakina gegoo
odoozhitoonaawaa. Owenipanendaanaawaa dash
wiinawaa iw.

Gii-gichi-anokiiwag iko anishinaabeg. Gii-pabaa-daawag
igaye idi. *Iskigamizigan* ogii-izhinikaadaanaawaa.
Mii idi na'inamowaad onow odaabajichiganiwaan,
weweni miinawaa iskigamizigewaad miinawaa.
Iskigamiziganing ezhinikaanaawaad. Ini-nitaawigiwaad
igo mii ge wiinawaa miinawaa ani-izhichigewaad
igo mii go miinawaa da-aabajitoowaad iniw ayi'iin
iw. Mii-go idi gaa-pabaa-daawaad iko anishinaabeg
iskigamizigewaad. Chi-neniibowa ogii-ozhitoonaawaa:
ziinzibaakwad, zhiiwaagamizigan miinawaa
ziiga'igaansan.

My mom and them used to throw butter into the kettle, while we were cooking the sugar, when we made sugar. They'd make these little wooden containers when they finished the sugar, sugar cakes, and syrup.

We knew how much snow to use to get the sugar to the right consistency. We used snow until it got done. Also, you shouldn't burn it. You shouldn't burn it. We knew how much to cook it when we wanted to make something.

It was a lot of work. Hardly anyone does that anymore. The white people have made all the things to make it easy. They think it's easy.

But the Indians used to work really hard. They also used to live around there. They call it *iskigamizigan,* or *sugar camp.* That's where they stored all their tools for when they make maple sugar again [for the next sugar season]. They call this *iskigamizigan,* or the *sugar camp.* When they grow up, they'll do the same thing and use the same things. The Indians used to live around there when they were boiling sap. They made a lot of each: sugar, syrup, and sugar cakes. So that's all I know about maple sugar.

Mii i'iw eta ezhi-gikendamaan iw ziinzibaakwad.
Imaa-sh ige ingii-kagwejimigoo i'iw, aaniin
gaa-onji-maajitaad a'aw anishinaabe gaa-izhi-mikang
i'iw iskigamizigeng i'iw. Gaa-izhi-noondamaan-sa,
aw baapaase giiwenh a'aw Wenabozho-sh igo imaa
dibaajimaa aw. Amanj imaa gaa-izhichigewaagwen.
Gaawiin weweni ingikendanziin i'iw. Mii gegaa
Wenabozho-go gaa-gikendamogwen i'iw.

Miigwech. Mii-sa eta minik gaye
niin gekendamaan. Mii azhigwa
chi-aya'aawiyaan ayigwa.

That's all I know about maple sugar. And also they asked me how the Indians started making maple sugar, how the Indians discovered making sugar. They way I heard it was that it had to do with the woodpecker, and Wenabozho is mentioned too. I don't know what they did. I don't really know it too good. Wenabozho must've known somehow.

Thank you. This is all I know about this. I am an elder now.

Ji-bagijiged O-miigaazod

Mezinaashiikwe indizhinikaaz. Iwidi ayi'iing, indoonjibaa Gaa-zagaskwaajimekaag. Oodi-go keyaa Gwiiwizensiwi-zaaga'iganiing ingii-tazhi-nitaawig. Idi keyaa wenjibaayaan. Miinawaa bangii omaa gegoo ji-ikidoyaan iidog, asemaa ji-dazhimag. Gabe-ayi'ii gaye niin azhigwa imbimaadiz. Ingichi-aya'aaw ayigwa. Azhigwa ba-izhi-gikendamaan a'aw asemaa, omaa inga-dibaajim.

Omaa gii-maajaawaad ongow indawemaag o-miigaazowaad 1945, chi-niibowa gii-maajaawag gwiiwizensag gii-o-miigaazowaad. Mii-sh imaa endaayaang nimaamaa endaad, niibowa omaa, mii imaa ingiw onji-maajaawaad ingiw gwiiwizensag Gwiiwizensiwi-ziibiing imaa akina gii-ayaawaad.

Mii-sh imaa nimindimooyenyag imaa gii-ayaawaad, ayigwa imaa gii-maajaawaad. Mii-sh aw bezhig mindimooyenh gaa-inaad iniw gwiiwizensan, "Gego, gego nibiikaang miigaazokegon. Gego giga-bi-azhegiiwem akina." Mii-sh iw geget gaa-izhichigewaad ingiw gwiiwizensag, indawemaag ige.

To Make an Offering When He Goes to War

My name is Mezinaashiikwe. I come from over there at Leech Lake. I was raised at Little Boy River, where I was raised. That's where I come from. I'm talking about tobacco. I have lived a long time. I am an elder. What I know about tobacco, I'm going to talk about here.

When my brothers left to go over to fight in 1945, there were many boys who left when they went over there to fight. We all gathered in my mother's house because there was a depot there (that's why they were there, they were getting on the train); lots of boys left from Little Boy River where they were all at. And there were old ladies there when they left. And one old lady said to those boys, "Don't fight in the water. Don't, and you will all come home." And that's what those boys did, and my brothers too.

Miinawaa ogii-inaan,
"Asemaa asig. Gichi-waasa
idi ga-izhaam. Gaawiin
gigikendanziinaawaa
aaniindi ge-izhaayeg
waa-izhinizha'ogooyeg
ji-o-miigaazoyeg. Mii apane
asemaa ge-zhi-aseg." Mii-sa
geget gaa-izhichigewaad.

Akina-sh indawemaag
gii-pi-azhegiiwewag. Niibowa
gii-pi-azhegiiwewag ingiw
anishinaabeg. Gaawiin igo
awiiya ingikenimaasiin imaa
gaa-gikenimag gii-aapidendid. Geget mashkawizii aw
asemaa.

Chi-mookomaan ogii-ozhi'aan iniw asemaan. Awedi-sh
chi-mewinzha anishinaabeg ogii-ozhi'aawaan
iniw asemaan. Ingikendaan iko gii-ozhi'aawaad
ingichi-anishinaabemag.

Bijiinag-sh igo ge wiinawaa asemaa. Mii-sh igo ge wiin
igo aw asemaa ezhi-mashkawiziid.

And she said to them, "Put down tobacco. You all are going far away. You don't know where you're going to go fight. Always put down tobacco." That's what they did.

My brothers came back home. There were many Indians who came back home. I don't know anybody who I know who didn't come back. Tobacco is pretty strong.

The white man made the tobacco. But a long time ago the Indians made their own tobacco. I know that my elders used to make tobacco. Later on they knew about the *asemaa* that you buy now. Tobacco is strong.

Agoodwewin

Miinawaa iko aw nishiime, Julia gii-izhinikaazo.
Maajaayaang iko babaa-agoodooyaang waaboozoog.
Idi miikanaang megwaayaak imbimibizomin
igo. Gii-ishpatemagad igo. Agoodooyaang,
ayi'ii iw biiwaabikoons ayaabajitooyaang.
Ninitaa-agoodoomin-sago.

Mii-sh ayigwa, miinawaa, gii-waabang miinawaa,
aangodinong-go niizhogon, niizhogon bijiinag
ninaadagwemin.

Maajaayaang naadagweyaang. Mii-sh igo miinawaa
nagwaanangidwaa ingiw waaboozoog. Aangodinong
niswi ninagwaanaag. Aw nishiime, iwidi ge wiin
bakaan dazhi-agoodoo. Ayaa
idi waabamag biijibatood mii
gaa-pi-baabiibaagid. Mii nawaj
wiin niibowa gii-nagwaanaad.
Weweni iko giiweyaang
napodinikeyaang.

Snaring

My younger sister, her name was Julie. We would go out and snare rabbits. We drive out on the country roads. There was a lot of snow. We use that wire to make snares. We know how to set snares.

The next day, sometimes we don't go check our snares for two days. We go check our snares. We caught some rabbits. Sometimes I catch three. My sister, she set her snares in different spots. We come out to the road and she was running and hollering at me, hollering. She caught more than I did. We'd go home, cook it, and make dumplings.

Gii-pi-bajiishka'ondwaa

Maazhaa gaye ingii-naano-biboonagiz
gii-maaminonendamaan enakamigak.
Gii-agaashiinyiwiyaang iko iwidi gaa-taayaang idi
Gwiiwizensiwi-zaaga'iganiing idi ingii-taamin.
Imbaabaa ogii-ozhitoon idi ayi'ii, waakaa'igan. Mii
iwidi miinawaa apane gii-ayaayaang. Aw nishiime
ge wiin gii-niiyo-biboonagizi. Miinawaa ikwezens
gii-niso-biboonagizi. Aanish idi gaa-inakamigak
igo, gii-taawag igo imaa anishinaabeg ingiw imaa
jiigi-zaaga'igan. Ingoding igo maaminonendamaan
imbizindawaag iko ingiw gaagiigidowaad. Ayaapii-go
ingii-nisidotam igo. Awiiya giiwenh idi wii-pi-izhaad.
Gichi-odaabaan idi wii-pi-izhaa. Mii-sh apane giiwenh
wii-pimi-mashkikiikaanigooyaang ayi'ii *Chicken Pox*
ganabaj gii-pajiishka'ogooyaang. Mii apane nimaamaa
imbaabaayiban apane maajaawaad. Ozhitoowaad
iwidi gii-asind a'aw waakaa'iganing igo imaa-go
mashkikiiwininiwag bajiishka'ogooyaang.

When They Came to Give Them Shots

I was maybe about five years old when I realized what was going on. When I was little, we lived at Boy Lake. My dad built a house. We were always over there. My little brother was four years old. And my little sister was three years old. Well it happened over there. The Indians lived near the lake. Once I realized that something was happening, I would listen to them talking. I understood once in a while. Someone apparently was coming. A big vehicle was coming. They always wanted to come by to inoculate us, with a shot for chicken pox, I think. My mom and dad left. They made a house out there, and people were put in that house when the doctors gave us shots.

Gigizheb nimaamaanaan gii-piindiged
ayigwa gii-ozhiitaa'iyangid. Bakwezhiganan
igaye zaasakokwaanan igaye omaajiinaan.
Gii-maajiizhiyangid megwaayaak gii-izhiwizhiyangid
nimaamaanaan. A'aw gaa-izhiyangid, "Gego
ji-bajiishka'ogoosiwaang." Mii enendang, mii giiwenh
bi-nisindwaa ingiw anishinaabe bi-nisigooyaang
wii-pi-bajiishka'ogooyaang. Shot was to save us [from]
Small Pox. Mii idi gii-kaazhiyangid aw nimaamaa,
maamaanaan.

Miinawaa wayaabang, noondawangidwaa
baa-baabiibaagiwaad imbaabaayiban miinawaa
nisayenyag mii gaa-izhi-mikaagooyaang ayigwa.
"Geyaabi-na gii-bimaadiziwag," indinendam.
Gii-maajiinigooyaang iwidi gii-izhiwinigooyaang gaye
niinawind ji-pajiishka'ogoowaang. Enda-baataniinowag
idi wayaabishkiiwejig, chi-mookomaanag ge
imaa niibawiwag. Baataniinowag abinoojiinyag.
Gaganawaabamangidwaa ingiw Wayaabishkiiwejig. Mii
iidog gii-nibowaad. Mii iidog minik gaa-pajiishka'onjig,
mii gii-nibowaad. Mii wenji-waabishkiziwaad.
Nimaamaa chi-gaaskanazootawag, "Maam, mii-na
gii-niboyan?" "Gaawiin," ikido. Mii gaye niinawind
gii-pajiishka'ogooyaang abinoojiinyiwiyaang.
Gii-kiiweyaang, weweni gii-izhi-ayaayaan.

Mii iw bezhig gaa-izhiwebak.

My grandmother came in early and got us ready. She took along bread and frybread. She took us out to the woods and my grandmother told us: "Don't let them shoot us." That's what she thought, that the Indians were going to get killed by getting "shot." The shot was to save us from smallpox. That's when my mom and grandmother hid us out there.

Then the next day, I heard my dad and older brothers hollering around for us, and that's when they found us. I was thinking, "Are they still alive?" They took us away, taking us to get a shot. There were a lot of white people standing around there. And a lot of children. I looked at those white people. They must've died. All the ones who got shots, they died. That's why they're white. I whispered to my mom, "Did you die?" "No," she said. We all got shots too when we were kids. We went home and we were okay.

That's one that happened.

43

Gii-twaashin Mikwamiing

Mii iw bezhig gaa-izhiwebak. Miinawaa-sh imaa mii-go
ayaapii-go gaawiin nimikwendanziin. Gii-piboon
idi. Agaami-zaaga'igan iwidi, gii-piboon idash,
gii-ayaamagad idi *a logging camp.* Gii-tebaabandamaan
iko iwidi endazhi-anokiiwaad ingiw ininiwag,
lumber camp. Iwidi indebaabamaanaanig
ingiw bebezhigooganzhiig. Bangii-go imaa
indebaabamaanaanig apane waasechigan. Iniw
mitigoon ingiw bebezhigooganzhiig azhewinaawaad
iwidi ayi'iing oodenaang endazhi-giishka'aakwewaad.
Ingoding igo miinawaa-go bemaadizijig imaa eyaajig
gaa-izhi-maajaawaad niibawiwaad idi jiigibiig
inaabiwaad iwidi. Mii ge niin iwidi inaabiyaan
idi bebezhigooganzhiig gii-twaashinowaad.
Chi-mamaandidowag ingiw bebezhigooganzhiig.
Gaa-izhi-dwaashinowaad.

He Fell through the Ice

That's one thing that happened. Sometimes I don't
remember. It was winter over there. Across the lake, it
was winter, there was a logging camp. I used to look
over there where the men were working at the lumber
camp. We saw the horses over there. We barely saw
them from the window. The horses were taking the
logs back to town to the sawmill. Sometime later some
people who were there left and were standing on the
beach looking out there. I was looking too when the
horses fell through the ice. The horses were really big.
And so they fell through the ice.

Mii i'iw bezhig idash gaawiin ogii-gashki'aasiwaawaan.
Mii imaa gii-kibwanaabaawed a'aw bebezhigooganzhii
bezhig. Amanj idash igo dasogon ayigwa miinawaa
ongow ikwewag baapinakamigiziwaad ozhiitaawaad.
Gaye wiinawaa nimaamaa ozhiitaad. Ayi'ii,
mookomaan omaajiidoon miinawaa waagaakwad.
Miinawaa ge gii-maajaawaad. Amanj gaa-tashiwaagwen
ingiw ikwewag. Mii idi gaa-izhaawaad iwidi a'aw
bebezhigooganzhii gii-kibwanaabaawed. Mii iwidi
mashkawaakwajid a'aw bebezhigooganzhii. Mii idi
nimaamaa ingiw ikwewag gaa-izhaawaad idi iniw
bebezhigooganzhiin. Gii-ayaamowaad iw ge wiiyaas
bebezhigooganzhii. Gii-ayaamowaad gii-piidoowaad
wiiyaas bebezhigooganzhii. Gaye wiin nimaamaa
gii-piidood. Amanj iidog keyaa gaa-izhitoogwen
gii-kiizizang i'iw bebezhigooganzhii-wiiyaas.
Nimaamaa ge wiin ogii-piidoon niibowa. Amanj iidog
ge gaa-miijiwaanen.

Mii i'iw gaa-izhichigewaad ingiw chi-anishinaabeg i'iw
eko-gikendamaan gii-abinoojiinyiwiyaang.

But they couldn't get one out. That horse drowned in there. I don't know how many days had gone by when these women got excited and got ready. My mom got ready too. She took a knife and an axe. And went over there too. I don't know how many women there were. They went over there where that horse drowned. It was frozen solid. My mom and those women went over there to that horse. They got some of it and brought back some horse meat. My mom brought some home too. I don't know what they did with it or how they cooked that horse meat. I don't know if I ate some or not.

That's what the elders used to do and what I know about it when we were kids.

Shut Up!

Gii-abinoojiinyiwiyaang, ingii-ashi-niiwimin. Ingiw-sh
memaandidojig, ayi'ii maajaawag. Gaawiin gaye niin,
onzaam ingii-agaashiinh, ingii-gikenimaasiig ingiw
zeziikizijig gikinoo'amaadiiwigamigong gii-izhaawaad.
Bakaan gaye niinawind ingii-agaashiinyimin.
Miinawaa ingii-naano-biboonagiz. Miinawaa nishiime,
gii-niiyo-biboonagizi. Miinawaa aw bezhig ikwezens—
gwiiwizens aw gaa-niiyo-biboonagizid—ikwezens dash
gii-niso-biboonagizi. Aw dash egaashiinyid nishiime,
gii-piibiiwi.

Ingoding igo idi gaa-taayaang ayi'iing
Gwiiwizensiwi-ziibiing.

Ingoding igo baamaa-go baandiganind ikwezens,
oshkiniiigikwe, aw chi-mookomaanikwe. Maagizhaa-sh
a'aw nimaamaa gaawiin ingii-wiindamaagosiinaan.
Ingii-agaashiinyimin. Gaawiin gegoo
ingii-pizindanziimin. Mii aw ingwana nimisenaan
a'aw, dagoshing gikinoo'amaadiiwigamigong.
Dagoshing ganawaabamangid chi-mookomaanikwens
imaa biindiged—chi-mookomaanikwe. Meta-go
zhaaganaashiimod. Gaawiin ninisidotawaasiwaanaan.
Meta-go niinawind gii-ojibwemoyaang
gii-abinoojiinyiwiyaang.

Shut Up!

When we were kids, there were fourteen of us. As for the bigger ones, they left. I too, because I was small, didn't know the oldest ones when they went to school. We were different ages. I was five years old. And my younger sibling was four. And another little girl—the little boy was the one who was four years old—but the little girl was three years old. My youngest sibling was just a baby.

One time we were living at Little Boy River. Sometime later a little girl was brought in, a young woman

rather, a white woman. Maybe my mother didn't tell us. We were small. We didn't listen to anything. It turned out to be our oldest sister arriving from school. When she arrived, we watched this little white woman come in—a white woman. She only spoke English. We didn't understand her. We only spoke Ojibwe when we were kids.

Mii-sh gii-piindigegozid ayigwa,
apane zhaaganaashiimod,
ganawaabamangid apane.
Aaniish naa ninishigiiwanizimin
gii-agaashiinyiwiyaang
abinoojiinyag ge-izhichigewaad.
Gwaakwaashkwaniyaang
di-nibaaganing idi
gaagiimaabamangid a'aw
ikwe, chi-mookomaanikwe.
Indoombiigizimin igaye
odaminoyaang. Mii-sa apane
eta-go izhiyangid i'iw, "Shut up!" indigonaan.
Mii-sago apane ezhiyangid i'iw. Gaawiin
ninisidotawaasiwaanaan i'iw wegonen wenji-ikidod
"Shut up!"

Azhigwa-sa gegapii-go azhigwa gaagiimaabamangid iko
nishigiiwaniziyaan. "Shut up," indinaanaan iko. Mii
iw ezhinikaazod gaa-inendamaang, *Shut Up*. Bijiinag
shago ingii-ni-gikinoo'amaagonaan i'iw. Bangii-go
naa gegoo gii-ni-gikendamaang zhaaganaashiimong.
Shke eniwek i'iw gegoo gii-gikendamaan
ayigwa mayaajii-gikinoo'amaagoowaang
gikinoo'amaadiiwigamigong gii-izhaayaang.
Ingii-paataniinomin igo abinoojiinyag, anishinaabensag
gaye, naa chi-mookomaanenzhishag. Mii-go naa
eniwek i'iw gii-ni-nisidotamaang i'iw. Meta-go
gii-ojibwemoyaang. Mii-sh iw geyaabi ojibwemoyaan.
Gaawiin wiikaa niwanendanziin, niwanitoosiin i'iw
indoojibwemowin.

And then when she moved in, she spoke English all
the time, and we looked at her all the time. After all,
we raised hell when we were little doing what children
do. We were jumping on the bunk bed in there keeping
an eye on that woman, that white lady. We were loud
too when we played. So she would always tell us,
"Shut up!" She would always tell us that. We didn't
understand why she was saying, "Shut up!"

We finally got caught peeking around over there
when we used to raise hell. We'd tell her, "Shut up!"
We thought that was her name, Shut Up. She taught
us what it was later. We learned a little bit at a time
to speak English. We learned more things after we
started going to school. There were a lot of us children,
little Indian kids and little white kids. We started to
understand more. We only spoke Ojibwe. But I still
speak Ojibwe. I haven't ever forgotten it nor have I ever
lost my Ojibwe language.

Bagida'waang Zaaga'iganiing

Akawe omaa inga-tibaajim ayi'iing indoonjibaa
ayi'iing Gaa-zagaskwaajimekaag. Iwidi keyaa ayi'iing
Gwiiwizensiwi-ziibiing ingii-tazhi-nitaawigimin.
Mezinaashiikwe indizhinikaaz. Miinawaa adik
indoodem. Mii-sh i'iw egooyaan omaa ji-dibaajimoyaan
o'ow bagida'waawin, ji-dazhindamaan.

Chi-mewinzha-sh igo idi inga-onji-maajitaa
gii-abinoojiinyiwiyaan gaa-izhichigewaad ingiw
anishinaabeg. Ogii-ozhi'aawaan iniw odasabiiwaan
ikwewag, iniw gaye ayi'iin agwanji'onaaganan.
Miinawaa iniw asiniin gii-aabaji'aawaad.
Gii-gichi-anokiiwag-sago. Gaye niin ingii-izhichige.
Nimaamaa ingii-gikinoo'amaag akina gegoo
gii-pagida'waayaan. Chi-anokiiwin igo iw. Gaawiin
geyaabi awiiya izhichigesiin i'iw. Noongom
bagida'waawaad, meta-go chi-mookomaan asabiin
iniw ayaabaji'aawaajin miinawaa bimibizowaad.
Ingii-chiimemin iko niinawind gii-pagida'waayaang
nimaamaa. Ogii-ozhi'aan iniw asabiin.
Dakobinangidwaa ingiw asabiig ani-onaagoshig
bagida'waayaang. Miinawaa gigizheb naadasabiiyaang.
Mii anooj awiiya giigoonyag ingii-tebibinaanaanig.
Mii miinawaa naadasabiiyaang, mii miinawaa
agoonangidwaa ingiw asabiig. Mii-go miinawaa mii-go
naasaab ezhichigeyaang endaso-giizhigak.

Fishing with a Net on a Lake

I'm going to tell a story here. I'm from Leech Lake.
We grew up toward Little Boy River. My name is
Mezinaashiikwe. People call me Dorothy Whipple. My
real name is Dora Whipple Mitchell, from the Mitchells
up there. And my clan is the Reindeer. And they told
me to tell a story about netting, to talk
about it.

I'll start from a long time
ago when I was a kid, with
what the Indians did. The
women made their own
nets and their own floaters.
And they used rocks. It was
a lot of work. I used to do
it too. My mom taught me
everything about fishing
with a net. That's hard
work. But nobody does that
anymore. These days they only use the white man's
nets and use motor boats. We used to go by boat when
my mom and I set nets. She made her own nets. We
tied up our nets and set our nets toward evening. And
in the morning, we go after our nets. We'd catch all
kinds of fish. And when we go after our nets, we hang
up the nets. We do it over every day.

Gii-nitaawichige aw nimaamaa akina gegoo.
Ogii-abwenaawaan ige iniw giigoonyan. Anooj-sago
ogii-izhi'aawaan iniw ayi'ii giigoonyan. Waawanoonsan
igaye gii-kiizizang iko nimaamaa.

Ayi'iing iwidi, Gwiiwizensiwi-zaaga'iganiing
iko idi ingii-pagida'waamin igaye. Mii idi
gaa-tazhi-nitaawigiyaang.

Gaye niin-sh igo azhigwa netaawigiyaan,
ayi'iing-ko ingii-pagida'waa iwidi chi-zaaga'igan
oodi Gaa-zagaskwaajimekaag. Chi-neniibowa iko
ingii-pagida'waamin. Chi-mookomaan asabiig
idash ingii-aabaji'aanaanig. Mii-go naaningodinong
ingodwaaswi ingii-o-bagida'waamin. Chi-neniibowa
giigoonyag. Dagwaagig mii-ko gii-pagida'waayaang.
Ingii-adaawaagemin ingiw naaningodinong
chi-neniibowa giigoonyag.

Mii iw. Miigwech.

My mom was good at everything. They also roasted the fish. They fixed the fish all kinds of ways. My mom also used to cook fish eggs. We used to set nets at Boy Lake too. That's where we grew up.

After I grew up, I used to go set net over there at the big lake, over at Leech Lake. We used to set a lot of nets. We use white man nets. Sometimes we set six nets. [We used to catch] a lot of fish. We set net in the fall. We also sometimes sold a lot of fish.

That's it. Thank you.

Wii-maji-doodawaad Awiiya A'aw Gookooko'oo

Akawe omaa gegoo niwii-tibaajim igo
gaa-apiichi-gikendamaan igo, gaa-izhiwebak iko
gii-abinoojiinyiwiyaan igo. Ingii-kezikwendaan igo iw.

Aya'aa, iwidi gii-taa a'aw nizhishenh. Bakaan idi gii-taa.
Gii-tani-go aw. Bebezhigooganzhiin ige ogii-ayaawaan
miinawaa-go baaka'aakwen. Gii-onizhishinini gaye
endaad a'aw nizhishenh. Onzaam ingii-paataniinomin
gii-abinoojiinyiwiyaang. Mii-sh aw imbaabaa
gaa-izhi-inaad: "Gaawiin abinoojiinyan ogii-ayaawaasiin
awiiya, Awenenan waa-ayaawaajin?" Gaa-izhi-miinaad igo
iniw oniijaanisan omaa iniw owiijiikiwenyan. Niin dash.
Amanj gaa-iniginiwaanen. Niin ingii-mamig. Ingii-pami'ig
ajina. Mii-sh i'iw gaa-izhi-gikendamaan eni-mindidoyaan
igo ayigwa gegoo gii-naanaagadawendamaan igo
enakamigak ezhichigewaad.

Apane idi gii-pi-noondaagozid a'aw gookooko'oo.
Endaso-dibik idi gii-pi-noondaagozid iwidi, iwidi
inzhishenh endaad. Mii gaa-izhi-nandomaawaad
iniw akiwenziiyan. Gii-chiisakii aw akiwenzii.
Gaa-izhi-nandomaawaad iwidi. Mii dash iwidi
gii-gikendang a'aw akiwenzii i'iw gaawiin gookooko'oo-go
aawisiin a'aw. Mashkiki awiiya owii-maji-doodaagoon
a'aw inzhishenh. Gaawiin geget gookooko'oo aawisiin
a'aw. Maji-mashkiki wii-toodaagod igo.

When the Owl Treated Someone Bad

I'm going to tell about how much I know, what happened when I was small. I barely remembered it.

My uncle lived over there. He lived someplace else. He was well off. He had horses and chickens. My uncle's house was nice too. There were too many of us when we were children. My dad said about him: "He doesn't have any children. Which one does he want?" And so he gave his brother that child. Me! I don't know how big I was. He took me. He took care of me for a little while. I figured it out as I got bigger when I thought about what happened and what they were doing.

That owl always made a screech. Every night that owl could be heard at my uncle's house. That's when they called for that old man to come out. He was a tent shaker. And so they invited him over there. Then that old man found out that it wasn't a real owl. Someone was sending bad medicine to my uncle. It wasn't a real owl. He was sent bad medicine.

Mii gaa-izhi-ikidod a'aw akiwenzii gaa-izhi-inaad
iniw, iniw bezhig oshki-ininiwan: "Daga akamaw
a'aw gookooko'oo." Mii geget gaa-izhi-akamawaad
a'aw oshki-inini gii-paashkizwaad gii-nisaad iniw
gookooko'oon. Mii iw wii-maji-doodawind gegoo
ji-wanitood iidog o'ow, o'ow eyaang maazhaa ge
ji-nibod. Gegaa-sago gii-nibod i'iw apii a'aw nizhishenh.
Gii-aakozi. Mii-sh i'iw gaa-ani-izhi-mino-ayaad.

Onzaam ingii-abinoojiinyiwimin, gaawiin
ingii-waabanda'igoosiimin a'aw gookooko'oo gaa-nisinjin.
Ingiw ininiwag-sago gii-paakinaawaad, mii-go giiwenh
eta-go bizhishig okanan a'aw gookooko'oo. Mii iw
mashkiki imaa gaa-izhi-biina'ang wiiyawining. Gaawiin
geget. Maji-aya'aawish a'aw awiiya.

Ke iko gaa-ayizhichigewaad ingiw anishinaabeg
gii-maji-doodaazowaad. Maji-mashkiki gii-aabajitoowaad.
Gaawiin geyaabi ingikendanziin awiiya ji-izhichiged
geyaabi. Niibowa iw, niibowa maji-mashkiki
ogii-aabajitoonaawaa. Miinawaa ayi'ii gaye
ataage-mashkiki ige gii-ayaamagad. Akina gegoo mashkiki
gii-ayaamagad.

Mii iw.

That's when the old man told a young man: "Go ambush that owl." Sure enough the young man ambushed that owl, shot it, and killed that owl. He was sent bad medicine so that he would lose what he has, or die. In fact, my uncle almost died at that time. He was sick. But then he got better.

Because we were kids, they didn't show us the owl that was killed. When those men opened that owl up, it was empty with just the bones of the owl. They had put that medicine in its body. It wasn't real. It was bad medicine.

That's the different things that the Indians did when they want to do harm to others. They used bad medicine. I don't know if anyone does that anymore. They used a lot of bad medicine. And there's even medicine for gambling. There's medicine for everything.

That's it.

Agoodweng Waaboozoon

Apane-ko gii-agoodooyaang. Ige, aanish naa
mashkawaakwajiwag ingiw. Giiwewinangidwaa
ingijiigibinaanaanig idash ingiw, weweni
biini'angidwaa. Nimaamaa-sako gii-izhichige. Mii-sh
aaningodinong anooj igo keyaa-go ogii-izhi'aan
giizizwaad. Ayi'iin ge ogii-saasakokwaanaan, miinawaa
napodiniked igaye, naboob ozhitood. Ayi'iin ge, oven
ige asaad.

Iko gii-abinoojiinyiwiyaang, ingii-kii'igoshimigoomin.

Chi-gigizheb mii-go agaawaa bi-waabang ayigwa
onishkaanaazha'ogooyaang. Ayi'ii akakanzhe
imaa atood nimaamaa, zhizhoobii'oyangid,
zaagijiwebinigooyaang gabe-giizhik. Gii'igoshimoyaang
iko, mii gaa-izhichigewaad anishinaabeg.

Snaring a Rabbit

We used to snare rabbits all the time. When you go find them, they're frozen. We would take them home, we would skin them, and we would clean them nice. My mom used to do that (that's how we learned that). She used to cook the rabbits all kinds of ways. She fried them and she made dumplings, making soup. She puts them in the oven.

When we were kids, we were put out to fast. They wake us up early in the morning, as dawn approached, and my mother put that black stuff [charcoal] on our faces and they would throw us out all day long. We fasted a lot, that's the way the Indians used to do that.

Iw gabe-giizhik babaa-ayaayaang megwaayaak,
aw nishiime anooj igo nishiimeyag miinawaa
cousins. Naanan igo ingoji babaa-ayaayaang
megwaayaak. Gaawiin indaa-wiisinisiimin. Gaawiin
igaye indaa-minikwesiimin gegoo. Baamaa idash
ingii-piibaagimigoomin-sago. Ke ingikendaamin-sago
apii ge-giiweyaang. Mii iw azhigwa nimaamaa ayigwa
jiibaakwed. Mii azhigwa ji-o-wiisiniyaang.

Mii-sh igo gaa-izhichigeyaang i'iw. Mii-sh aw nishiime,
gii-nibwaakaa. Mii gaa-izhi-agoodawangid aw waabooz
gii-izhinaazhikawangid imaa gii-nagwaanangid.
Gaa-izhi-boodaweyaang imaa gii-abweyaang
aw waabooz. Aanish naa ingii-maazhichigemin
iw gii-izhichigeyaang. Gii-wiisiniyaang idi.
Ingii-kagiibaadizimin gii-abinoojiinyiwiyaang.

Mii-sh ige aw aya'aa, chi-mookomaanag imaa
gii-ayaawag—*farmer*—eighteen kids ogii-ayaawaan.
Ge niinawind *fourteen* ingii-tashimin. Mii ingiw
gaa-wiiji'angijig apane,
chi-mookomaanag
abinoojiinyag.
Gaawiin ge wiikaa
ingii-miigaadisiimin-sago.
Anooj ingii-izhichigemin.

We stayed out in the woods all day long, with my youngest sister and brother, my nephews, and my cousins. There must have been about five of us hanging around in the woods. We weren't supposed to eat. We also couldn't drink anything. And later they'd call us when it was time to come home. We knew when it was time to come home. My mom cooks. We'll go and eat.

That's what we did. And my brother was real smart. We snared this rabbit, then we all got together, circled around that rabbit, and chased him into that snare and caught him. We built a fire and roasted the rabbit. We ain't supposed to do that. We did something bad when we did that. We ate out there. We were crazy kids.

There were people living there, our neighbors— a farmer with eighteen kids. There were fourteen of us. We played with those farmer kids, white kids. We never fought, we did a lot of things together.

Manoominike-zaaga'igan

Bangii miinawaa omaa gegoo niwii-tibaajim. Wawiyazh
igo gaa-izhiwebiziwaad. Ayi'iing iko idi ingii-taamin
Remer, Minnesota. Niibowa ingii-nitaawigi'aag
abinoojiinyag. *Uh grown up boys uh, uh, we used to
take two cars and about four canoes.*

Ayi'iing-sh iko idi ingii-o-manoominikemin, *East
Lake* izhinikaade. Anishinaabeg imaa daawag.
Ingii-inawemaanaanig omaa ingiw gaa-ayaajig.
Gaawiin awiiya imaa bakaan gii-piindiganaasiin
ji-manoominiked. Mii-sh iko idi ingii-nandomigoomin
iko idi ji-o-manoominikeyaang. Gaawiin ige
imaa awiiya gii-pagidinaasiin chi-mookomaan
ji-manoominiked.

Gii-kanawenjigaade iw. Mii ige ingiw *commitee*
oganawendaanaawaa apii ge-baakaakosing.
Gii-onizhishin i'iw manoomin.

Rice Lake

And now I'm going to tell another story. It was funny what happened to them. We used to live over there in Remer, Minnesota. I raised a lot of kids. Grown-up boys uh, uh, we used to take two cars and about four canoes.

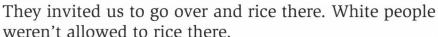

We used to go ricing over there at East Lake. There were Indians living there. We were related to the ones who were living there. They didn't bring anyone else in to rice there. They invited us to go over and rice there. White people weren't allowed to rice there.

It was taken care of by a committee, who decided when the lake would be open for ricing. The rice was good.

65

Mii-sh iko ge niinawind idi gaa-izhaayaang
o-manoominikeyaang. Mii-sh iwidi ingoding
ani-bagamibizoyaang, enda-niibowa idi niibawiwag idi.
Aya'aag ge imaa dakoniwewininiwag imaa niibawiwag
ani-baapiwaad. Chi-mookomaanag giiwenh owidi
megwaayaak keyaa gii-pi-izhaadog. Gii-pawa'amowaad
imaa. Mii gaa-izhi-zhizhoobii'odizowaad. Bekaa,
aaniin da naa ekidong? Ayi'iin ige iw, wiinizisimaanan
ogii-piizikaanaawaan. Gii-anishinaabe-zhizhoobii'odizo
waad miinawaa wiinizisimaanan gii-piizikamowaad.

Mii-sh ingiw imaa naagaanizijig imaa, babaa-ayaawag
ganawaabamaawaad iniw meta begidininjig
imaa ji-manoominikewaad. Gaawiin imaa awiiya
bakaan daa-manoominikesiin. Ozaagitoonaawaa iw
onizhishininig iw manoomin.

And so we went over there to rice. One time when we arrived there in the car, there were a whole lot of people standing there. Those game wardens were standing over there, laughing. Apparently white people had come here from over there through the woods. They were knocking rice there. They had painted themselves. Wait a second, how do they say it? And they were wearing wigs. They painted themselves like Indians and they wore wigs.

The head committee watched to see that only the ones who were allowed to rice would be ricing there. Nobody else could rice there. They were stingy with the good rice.

Mii-sh i'iw gaa-izhi-waabamaawaad iniw,
ogii-mayaginawaawaan iniw menoominikenijin.
Niizh iniw gaa-izhi-biminizha'waawaad, mii
aano-gii-kinjiba'igowaad idi megwaayaak
idi. Gaa-izhi-adimaawaad. Wegwaagi ingiw
chi-mookomaanag gii-shizoobii'odizowag.
Miinawaa iniw wiinizisimaanan gii-piizikamowaad
anishinaabewiwaad.

Mii iw.

And so they saw these strange-looking ricers. The two that they were chasing tried to run away into the woods. They caught them. And here, they were white guys who had painted themselves. And they wore wigs, trying to be Indians.

That's it.

Gii-maazhendam Gii-nanawizid

Omaa akawe gegoo inga-dibaajim gaa-izhiwebak iko.
Iwidi ingii-taamin iko idi ayi'iing, Remer idi. Aya'aa
dash i'iw, ingii-paataniinomin iko imaa gii-ayaayaang.
Mii-sh aya'aa, bezhig a'aw indinawemaagan
gaa-izhi-miizhid mayaajaad iniw odayan. Makadewizi
a'aw animoons. Giibaadiz gii-izhinikaazo. Aya'aa
ogii-nooji'aan iniw aya'aan zhaangweshiwan.

Mii-sh igo gii-maajiinaawaad
babaa-nandawaabamaawaad
iniw, mink iniw zhaangweshiwan.
Gii-ishpaginzo apii aw *that mink.*
Mii-sh iw gaa-inaabadizid a'aw, aw
animosh, babaa-andawaabamaad
iniw. Mii-sh i'iw gii-maajiinaawaad
iko ingiw gii-adaawamigoowaan
igaye, maajiinaawaad iniw
babaa-moonikaanaad iniw
zhaangweshiwan.

Ezhi-gikenimaad igo aaniindi
ayaanid. Mii-sh imaa waaniked imaa, mii-sh imaa inini
imaa namadabid. Mii-sh imaa namadabid besho inini,
mii-sh azhigwa besho gikenimaad ayaanid, mii azhigwa
migid. Mii-sh a'aw inini imaa ezhi-atood wanii'igaans.

He Was Upset When He Was Empty-Handed

I'm going to tell about something that happened. There were quite a few of us living there in Remer, Minnesota. My relative gave me his dog, a black puppy, after he left. His name was Giibaadiz. He hunted mink, he was a mink dog.

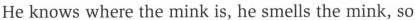

They used to come borrow this dog to go hunt mink. It was worth money at that time, that mink hide. They used him for hunting. They used to come borrow this dog from me to go hunt. They'd take him along to go dig the mink out.

He knows where the mink is, he smells the mink, so

he digs a hole while that man sits there. He's digging the hole and that man is sitting there. When he knows that mink is close, that dog barks. He [the man] puts a trap there.

Some of them would just catch him with leather gloves, just grab him, and pull him out of the hole. That's what the dog was for.

71

Aanind wiin igo
ogii-tebibinaawaan igo,
wiikobinaawaad imaa
waanikaaning. Mii
gaa-inaabadizid animosh.

Mii-sh azhigwa iko dagoshing,
enda-minwaabaawe giikajid.
Enda-minawaanigozi. Mii i'iw
gii-mikawaawaad iniw gii-nisaawaad bezhig.
Enda-minwendam iko. Giishpin awiiya mikawaasigwaa
awiiya nanawiziwaad, mii
enda-maazhendam dagoshing
wa'aw animoonzhish. Mii i'iw
azhigwa gawishimod.

Mii-sa eta-go omaa bangii
enaajimoyaan.

When he gets home, he's all wet and cold. He's just happy when he comes in, wagging his tail and happy. That means they found one, that they killed one. He's just happy. If they don't find one and come home empty-handed, he comes home sad, this poor little dog. When he comes home sad, he just lies down. That means they didn't get anything.

I'm just telling a little story here.

Ogii-miigaadaanaawaa I'iw Waazakonenjigan Imaa Atood Miinawaa Iw Aazhogan

Aanish niwii-tazhindaan imaa iw, imaa ayi'iing
Little Earth 1973 imaa *I've been living there.*
Mii-sh imaa niibowa imaa gii-niiwanishkoozowag.
Ingiw ge gaawashkwebiijig abinoojiinyag igaye
gii-bizikoozowag imaa ingiw. Gaawiin gegoo omaa
gii-ayaasinoon ji-noogishkaawaad ingiw odaabaanag
ji-gii-bizikoonaawaad.

They Fought to Have That Stoplight and Bridge Put In

And I am going to talk about there at Little Earth, where I've been living since 1973. There were a lot of people, Indians, who got killed there [before they put that stoplight up]. Kids and drunks got hit by cars. There wasn't anything here to stop the cars from hitting them.

Mii dash a'aw Clyde Bellecourt, *I admire him, he's a great man*. Mii a'aw gaa-atood imaa i'iw waazakonenjiganan. Apii gaa-izhiwebak i'iw, gichi-niibowa imaa anishinaabeg gii-ayaawag noogishkaa'aawaad iniw odaabaanan. Mii-sh i'iw dakoniwewininiwag ikonaazha'waawaad iniw anishinaaben imaa. Gaawiin igo gaye anishinaabeg, chi-mookomaanag igo ge imaa gii-wiidookaazowag gii-wiikwajitoowaad i'iw, omaa iniw waazakonenjiganan ji-atoowaad ji-noogishkaawaad ingiw odaabaanag. Mii-sh i'iw geget i'iw gii-gashkitoowaad i'iw, gii-achigaadeg idi. Ke gaye niin igo indizhaa apane idi. Ni-enda-minwendam igo imaa ge weweni imaa aazhawishkaayaan imaa.

Mii-sh i'iw geget gii-nichiiwakamigad-sago apii. Gaawiin niin imaa ingii-wiidookaazosiin. Apii-go idi ge niinawind ingii-onzaabimin. Ingii-kosaanaanig ingiw dakoniwewininiwag.

And Clyde Bellecourt, I admire him, he's a great man. He's the one who put in that stoplight. When all this happened, there were a lot of Indians stopping the cars. And then those cops chased off those Indians. Not just Indians, white people too helped out to try to put in that stoplight so the cars would stop. Eventually they were able to get it done over there, putting one in over there. I too go over there all the time. I'm glad I can walk through there too.

And there was really a big doings at the time. I didn't help out there. We watched from a distance. We were afraid of the cops. There are a lot of different people there. We were scared of them. My younger brother said for us not to go anywhere when they were protesting.

Geget igo, anooj igo awiiya geget iw, geget
baataniinowag ingiw. Nigosaanaan. Sago-nishiime
gaawiin ingii-ig iko aaniindi ji-izhaasiwaang imaa
gii-nichiiwakamigak.

Ke-sh niminawaanigwendam imaa babaa-ayaayaan.
Niibowa ikidowag gotamowaad imaa wii-ayaawaad.
Gaawiin niin. Niminwendam omaa ayaayaan. Gaawiin
ingoji indaa-izhi-gozisiin. Gaawiin. Bakaan iko
ingii-taa wayeshkad omaa babaa-ayaayaan. Gaawiin
ingii-minwendanziin. Weweni inganawenimigoomin
igaye gii-achigaadeg gegoo dekaag igaye. Weweni ge
giizhoozhiyaan azhigwa. Ingikaa ayigwa. Gaawiin
ingoji indaa-izhaasiin. Niminwendam omaa.

Niibowa noozhishenyag imaa indazhi-nitaawigi'aag.
Niibowa noozishenyag imaa
inganawenimaag. Mii-go geyaabi
apane eta-go bi-wiisiniwaad igo.
Naaningodinong iko ninoondese
iko. Mii-sh igo booch igo
gaawiin aanind ingoji ayaasiiwag
noozhishenyag.

Miigwech.

I'm glad to be around that area. A lot of people say they are afraid to be there. Not me. I like being here. I can't move anyplace else. No. I used to live in a different place at first. I didn't like it. They also take good care of us by bringing us ice cream. I keep warm where I'm at now. I'm getting old. I can't go anywhere else. I'm happy here.

I've raised quite a few of my grandkids there. I take care of a lot of them there. They still come in and eat. Once in a while, I run out of food. Sometimes my grandkids are not all here.

Thank you.

Imbiindaakoojige Imaa Asiniing

Bangii miinawaa omaa inga-dibaajim
gaa-izhiwebiziyaan.

Iwidi ingii-maajaa. Ingii-pimise gii-izhaayaan gii-o-
waabamag aw noozhishenh idi gikinoo'amawind,
Reno, Nevada. Mii idi gaa-izhaayaan chi-waasa.
Indaanis ingii-wiijiiwaa. Ingii-segiz imaa mayaajaayaan.
Sa-ingii-minwendam gii-o-waabamag aw noozhishenh.
Gikinoo'amawaa idi.

Mii-sh iwidi, gii-ni-ayaayaang idi Colorado. *We change
planes there.* Mii gaawiin ingoji ingii-waabandanziin
aki asemaa wii-o-asag. Mii-sh iwidi degoshinaan iwidi,
waa-pi-maajaayaang gii-izhiwinigooyaang idi miinawaa
ji-bi-azhegiiweyaang. Mii-sh idi gii-pabaamoseyaan
idi, baa-naanaagadawendamaan chi-waasa idi
babaa-ayaayaan chi-waasa akiing. Nimanidoowendam
idi ganawabandamaan i'iw aki. Mii-sh igo
gii-mikwenimagwaa ingiw. Chi-mewinzhakamig
anishinaabeg omaa gii-ayaadogenag gaye wiinawaa.
Miziwe gigii-ayaamin omaa akiing. Miziwe
anishinaabeg gii-ayaawag.

I Made an Offering There on the Rock

I'm going to tell a little story about what happened to me. I went over there. I flew when I went to see my grandchild, who is going to school over there in Reno, Nevada. I went far away. I took my daughter with me. I was scared when I left. I was glad to go see my grandchild. He goes to school over there.

We were over in Colorado. We change planes there. I didn't see any bare ground to go put down tobacco. After we arrived there, they took us to our connecting flight to come back home. I was walking around thinking when I was in a faraway land. I was thinking sacredly looking at that land. I was thinking about the people who lived there way before the white

man. Long time ago, there were probably Indians there too. We Indians were all over on this land. There were Indians all over.

Gaa-izhi-maajaayaan iwidi gii-nandone'amaan i'iw
biinakamigaag. Gii-o-gaagiigidoyaan asemaa gii-asag.
Mikwenimagwaa anishinaabeg imaa gii-ayaadogenag
ge wiinawaa, gii-asag aw asemaa gii-kaagiigidoyaan.
Mii ezhichigeyaan dibi-go ge-izhaayaan asemaa asag.
Ayi'iing igaye nibiikaang igaye, asemaa apane asag.
Gaawiin ige inzagaswaasiin. Mii-go ezhi-bimiwinag aw
asemaa.

Geget mashkawizii aw asemaa. Indebweyendam niin
i'iw asemaa aabaji'ag.

And so I got there and was walking around looking for clean ground. I went over to put down tobacco and talk with it.

I was thinking about that there were probably Indians who lived there, and I put down tobacco and spoke. That's what I do, anyplace I go I put down tobacco. And in the water also, I always put down tobacco. I never smoked in my life. I always carry tobacco. Tobacco is pretty strong. I believe in tobacco.

Chi-mewinzha iko ge wiin gichi-anishinaabeg
gii-tazhimaawaad iko asemaan. Ke-sh i'iw noongom
weshki-bimaadizijig gaawiin, gaawiin-sago gegoo
wii-pizindanziiwag. Meta-go wii-sagaswaanaawaad
asemaan. Gaawiin mewinzha-ko iw gii-izhichigesiiwag.
Gii-oshki-bimaadiziyaang, gaawiin wiikaa
ingii-sagaswaasiimin. Gaawiin wiikaa inzagaswaasiin.
Meta nimishoomis gaa-waabamag iko gii-sagaswaad
gii-abinoojiinwiyaan. Geget-sa indebwe ekidoyaan.

Miigwech.

84

Long ago the elders always talked about tobacco. Nowadays the young people don't want to listen to anything. All they wanted to do was smoke tobacco. Long ago they didn't do this. When we were young, we never smoked. I never smoked. The only one I ever saw smoke was my grandfather, when I was a child. It's true what I'm saying.

Thank you.

Makwa Ingii-pimaaji'ig

Niwii-tibaajim omaa gaa-izhiwebiziyaan.
Niizho-biboonagad gaa-ako-izhaayaan ayi'iing
Waashtanong idi ingii-izhaamin. Anishinaabeg
idi gii-maawanji'idiwaad. Miziwe gii-onjibaawag
anishinaabeg. Mii gaye niin idi gii-o-wiidookaazoyaan.
Indaanis idi ingii-wiijiiwaa. Mii idi ingiw niniijaanisag
ayi'iing, Seattle, mii idi gaa-tiba'angig. Gaye-sh idi
gaawiin-go weweni nimino-bimosesiin.

Mii-sh idi gaa-izhi-nakweshkawag a'aw. Aw indaanis
midewi aw indaanis. Niibowa ogikenimaan igo
iniw anishinaaben medewinijin miinawaa iniw
nenaandawi'iwenijin. Gaa-izhi-nakweshkawaad
iwidi bezhig ininiwan. Midewi aw inini.
Nanaandawi'iwe. Gaa-izhi-nandomaad. Aaniish naa
ingii-kagiibishe. Gaa-izhi-nandomaad iniw ininiwan
ji-nanaandawi'id aw inini. Mii-sa geget idi ayi'iing
baataniinowag anishinaabeg. Geget iwidi gii-ayaayaan,
gii-namadabiyaang, namadabiwag michayi'ii.
Ayigwa nagamod gaagiigidod a'aw asemaan imaa
odoopwaaganan odoopwaaganiwaan omaa asaawaad.
Mii-sh i'iw gii-kaagiigidod aw inini. Miinawaa aw
bezhig aw nagamo. Dewe'igaansan iniw baaga'waad
a'aw bezhig iniw wiijiiwaaganan. Nanaandawi'we idi
iidog a'aw inini.

Bear Saved My Life

Two years ago, I went to Washington, D.C., that Indian
Nations Centennial. There were a lot of Indians from all
over. I went to go help out too. Me and my daughter,
we went on a train. We stayed over there four days. My
kids over in Seattle are the ones who paid for us to go.
And that's when I lost my hearing.
I could hardly walk.

And so I met him [a medicine man] there. My daughter
is a *Midewi* woman [Mide lodge member]. She knows
a lot of people, *Midewi* people, medicine people. She
knows a lot of people from all over, because she goes
to those lodges, *Midewi* lodges, and gathers medicine.
And so she met this one man. I guess this guy was a
medicine man. He doctors people. So she invites him.
After all, I was deaf. So she invited this guy and his
friend to doctor me because of my legs. There really
were a lot of Indians. So we went to the park, there
was a lot of parks. They put a blanket on the ground
there, and put the pipes on there. There were two guys.
This guy was talking and smoking his pipe from where
he was sitting, and talking. While he was talking,
this other guy was pounding his hand drum. That
man doctors people. And I was sitting there, and my
daughter too, she was smoking her pipe.

Mii-sh i'iw gii-kiizhiitaad, indaano-gii-wiindamaag-sh
ge-izhichigeyaan i'iw nitawagan. Mii-sh imaa
gii-tibaajimod i'iw, gii-kagwejimid i'iw: "Awenen aw
gidoodem," indig. "Makwa."

Mii-sh i'iw ikidod i'iw, imaa namadabiyaan
gii-waabamaad iniw makwan imaa ishkweyaang
imaa namadabiwag. Omaa endazhigidaazod aw
makwa. Miinawaa idi inaabid idi gii-waabamaad iniw
mashkode-bizhiki. Imaa endazhigidaazod waaniked
miinawaa boopoodaajiged. Niin niwii-miigaanig.
Gegoo niwii-toodaag a'aw mashkode-bizhiki.
Ninishkaadenimig.

Mii dash aw makwa,
mii a'aw ozegi'aan. Mii
imaa endazhigidaazod
aw makwa, gaawiin
obagidinaasiin imaa besho
ji-bi-izhaanid. Mii i'iw
iidog a'aw indoodem imaa
gii-izhi-nanaandawi'iwed.
"Giga-mino-ayaa." Mii a'aw
makwa iidog genawenimid.

Mii iw.

Jonathan Reich

When the man got done, he tried to tell me what to do with my ear. Then he told a story, and asked me: "What is your clan?" "Bear."*

Then he said that where I'm sitting he saw that *makwa* [bear] sitting behind my back. He was real mad. He was mad. And he looked the other way, he saw this *mashkode-bizhiki* [buffalo]. He was just snarling, you know how a buffalo gets mad, pawing at the ground with its feet. He wanted to fight me. That buffalo wanted to do something to me. He was really mad at me.

And as for that bear, he scared him [that buffalo]. He said the bear was protecting me, so that buffalo won't come near me. He doctored me by the help of my clan. He told me I'd be okay. *Makwa* was protecting me. He's my *doodem*.

That's it.

---

*In her later life, Dorothy has begun identifying herself by her mother's clan—Makwa. Her father was Caribou.

Notes on Orthography

Listeners of the audio recordings will notice that Dorothy uses reduced forms of many Ojibwe function words. For examples, the discourse particle *idash* 'as for, but' is reduced to *-sh*, and demonstratives such as *a'aw* 'that one' are reduced to *aw*. In these transcriptions, however, we elected to use full forms or semi-full forms for these types of reductions. Instead of Dorothy's extreme reduced form *a-* (what we refer to as *extreme clitics*, or words phonologically reduced to a point that they show severely reduced or no stress and that phonologically attach themselves to host words), *a'aw* or *aw* 'that one' (animate) is used. Full forms *i'iw* or *iw* 'that one' (inanimate) are used instead of extreme clitic form *i-*, and so on. The third-person animate demonstrative *a-* in Dorothy's phrase *a-nimise* 'my older sister' is inflated to *aw nimise* or *a'aw nimise* in the transcriptions.

This approach has both benefits and drawbacks. From a literary perspective, full forms of function words would be expected and appropriate, since the use of reduced forms, at least in the English literature tradition, results in what is perceived as a less formal work. It remains to be seen whether this is true or appropriate for Ojibwe literary publications. In other words, can certain *perceived* reductions in Dorothy's speech, such as the reduction in the first-person prefix *nin-* 'I' to just the nasal consonant *n-* be considered a reduction? Should the first-person prefix *nin-* (which occurs just as nasal consonant *n-* in certain linguistic environments for Dorothy) in her phrase *ngii-pizindawaag* 'I listened to them' be inflated to full form *ningii-pizindawaag* or to the less full form *ingii-pizindawaag*? Dorothy's speech patterns showed no evidence of a full form *nin-* (the personal prefix taught in school or at college to virtually all students of Ojibwe) before the past-tense marker *gii-,* even during redictation, where she repeated phrases slowly and deliberately. In fast speech, there was no evidence of the vowel-initial variant *in-* 'I' before the past-tense marker *gii-* (past tense), i.e., not *ingii-,* but *ngii-.*

For *Chi-mewinzha,* we elected to follow, with caution, the convention of inflating words to their full forms. We inflate the personal prefixes in phrases such as Dorothy's *ngii-pizindawaag* 'I listened to them' to the initial vowel variant *ingii-pizindawaag,* not to *ningii-pizindawaag,* since there is at least some evidence that Dorothy brings back the elided initial vowels in certain words, like *zhigwa,* that were inflated to full form (*azhigwa* 'now') during redictation. From a literary point of view, this is acceptable. From a language learning point of view, representing only full forms, or less full forms, can be misleading to students of Ojibwe, because frequently the goal when studying Ojibwe is to speak like native speakers. Language learners who make it a practice to study transcriptions (and many students do) might get the impression that Dorothy speaks only in full forms, and as a result will attempt to speak Ojibwe (as part of their learning process) in only full forms. My personal concern is that students might not ever use *a-nimise* (with extreme clitic *a-* [third-person animate demonstrative]) in their speech patterns if they are not aware that such extremely reduced forms exist. The printed word is very powerful, and many students tend to revere the printed word (albeit inadvertently) over the actual performance of the native speaker. Sometimes students see full forms such as *a'aw nimise* in the transcription, but they do not notice that it occurs as severely reduced, i.e., *a-nimise,* in the actual speech of the native speaker in the audio. Because we anticipate that students will study these transcriptions as part of their Ojibwe language learning and that these stories might be used in classrooms, we emphasize this point here.

Students accustomed to reading Ojibwe transcriptions will notice a few differences in hyphenation in these transcriptions. The convention has been to use hyphens in writing Ojibwe to separate prefixes or preverbs from their host words, i.e., *ingii-pizindawaag* 'I listened to them' as opposed to *ingiipizindawaag*, or, in compound-type words, to separate certain morphemes, i.e., *maji-mashkiki* 'bad medicine'. The function of hyphens in writing Ojibwe has been to show a loose connection between various constituents within a word complex. Hyphens have not previously been used to show loose connections of clitics as we have done in these transcriptions. For example, *mii-sh* 'and then, and as for' has usually been represented in many Ojibwe transcriptions as just *miish* 'and then'. We know that *miish* is really a combination of two words, discourse marker *mii* 'that, now, really' and second-position particle *idash* 'but'. While *idash* may occur as reduced form *dash*, i.e., *mii dash*, it may also occur as extreme clitic *-sh*. Because it is helpful for language learners to be aware of these types of loose connections between words such as *mii* and *idash*, we go against convention here and use a hyphen to make the relationships between words like *mii* and extreme clitics such as *-sh* more explicit. This practice approximates the tendency of native speakers to group such words and their clitics together in this fashion. For example, Mille Lacs Band Ojibwe elder Millie Benjamin used to write phrases such as *mii-go ge-zhi-wawaabishkiganzhiiyan*, as it would be written in the orthography of this book, simply as *miigo gezhi-wawaabishkiganzhiiyan* 'You'll have tell-tale white spots on your fingernails'. Millie did not use hyphens, but we can easily see how she grouped her words together, especially clitic words like *-go*. The traditional convention has been to leave a space between *mii* and emphatic particle *go*, i.e., *mii go ge-zhi-wawaabishkiganzhiiyan*. To more fully approximate native speaker groupings such as Millie's, we use hyphens.

We hope that the orthography may be adapted and modified as needed to represent our increasing knowledge of the Ojibwe language and its linguistic features. The orthography in these transcriptions is meant to represent such new knowledge and understanding.

Transcription Notes

Brendan Fairbainks

These stories were told to Wendy Geniusz by Dorothy Dora Whipple, a native speaker from the Leech Lake Reservation in northern Minnesota. Most of these stories were digitally recorded on video or audio tapes. Two of these stories were recorded on analogue tapes and digitized. Wendy transcribed most of these stories from the original audios and film. As part of the transcription process, Wendy revisited Dorothy on various occasions for redictation. During redictation, Wendy played the original audio back to Dorothy, who immediately repeated what was said and provided a translation. This was also recorded. I subsequently reviewed the original audios, the recorded redictations, and Wendy's original transcriptions, to which I made appropriate corrections and adjustments. I also transcribed some stories that were not yet transcribed by the time I received Wendy's transcriptions. Based on these recordings, my job was to finalize these transcriptions for publication, which entailed checking the accuracy of the transcription against the audio, checking translations, and providing translations that were not offered by Dorothy in her redictation. For those stories without a redictation session, I checked questionable passages with consultant native speakers of Ojibwe. The Leech Lake native speakers we consulted were Johnny Mitchell (Bezhigoogaabaw), Delores Wakefield, Gerry Howard (Niingaabii'anook), Leona Wakonabo (Bizhiikiis), and Larry Smallwood (Amikogaabaw) from the Mille Lacs Band of Ojibwe reservation in east central Minnesota. Under normal circumstances, consultation with the original speaker is most desirable, with the original speaker authorizing all changes and maintaining control over the accuracy of the transcriptions. Unfortunately, Dorothy had become completely deaf by the time these transcriptions were finished and finalized for *Chi-mewinzha,* and we chose to confer with other native speakers to spot check when redictation sessions were not attached to a particular story. John Nichols graciously reviewed the transcriptions and offered many valuable comments and suggestions.

Given the task of finalizing these transcriptions for publication, I made decisions about how the redictation process ultimately would be used, since many of the more complex passages were changed during redictation. This affected Dorothy's original performance. In case the original audio files will be released or made available to the public, I used the redictation process only to clarify any questions of accuracy of the transcriptions based on her original performance. My approach was that of many editors and proofreaders: *only change something if it's wrong.* Dorothy was the only one who could determine whether a phrase was wrong or incorrect, so we let her make those judgments. Her original performance is the definitive version, and I inserted a redictated phrase only if it replaced an incorrect or undesired passage (i.e., where she replaced an English word with an Ojibwe one) or if she made significant changes to her own passages. My ultimate goal was not to leave the reader wondering why the printed text sometimes differs from what is actually heard in the audio files; my notes here explain these differences. Many of these notes provide alternate phrasings mentioned by Dorothy during redictation. Certain obvious repetitions or false starts in the text were deleted without acknowledgment in the notes.

Ogii-waabamaawaan Chi-ozagaskwaajimen
They Saw a Big Leech

Paragraph 1

[Aaniish]
 Johnny Mitchell suggested that the first word is *aaniish*. In
 many of her stories, Dorothy uses the reduced form *aansh*. The
 full form is used here.

Paragraph 2

[Aaniish naa mii imaa gaa-taawaad anishinaabeg.]
 False start deleted: *Mii iwidi . . .*

[Ogijayi'ii imaa gii-pi-mookiid imaa zaaga'iganiing.]
 False start deleted: *Gii-pi-mookiid . . .*

[Mii-sa iw]
 Johnny Mitchell replaced what sounds like *miish uh* with *mii-sa
 iw.*

Paragraph 3

[That's when the leech disappeared.]
 Literally, they raised the leech up into themselves.

Bagijigeyan Asemaa
When You Make a Tobacco Offering

Paragraph 1

[Mii iidog miinawaa omaa ji-dazhimag a'aw asemaa.]
 Redictated sentence inserted and sentence from audio deleted:
 Mii maa geyaabi maa ji-dazhimag ayi'ii-dog aw asemaa.

[Ongow animikiig bi-ayaawaad ayigwa, mii-sh giiwenh asemaa, asemaa ji-asang.]
  Deleted in redictation: *i'iw*.

[Mii-sh niin ezhichigeyaan i'iw, asemaa aw asag agwajiing biinakamigaag aw gaagiigidoyaan.]
  Redictated sentence not inserted: *Mii-sh niin i'iw ezhichigeyaan aw asemaa asag agwajiing biinakamigaag.*

Paragraph 2

[Ke-sh gaye niin azhigwa chi-aya'aawiyaan.]
  In redictation, Dorothy used *ayigwa* instead of *azhigwa*: *Ke-sh gaye niin ayigwa chi-aya'aawiyaan.*

Paragraph 4

[Ina, ke gosha, mii omaa aw asemaa, mii omaa apane aw asemaa bemi-ondinang.]
  False start deleted: *mii imaa gidanishinaabeminaanig.*

Paragraph 5

[Mii giiwenh iw dagwaagig, oshki-aya'aansag ingiw,]
  Deleted false starts: *ishkwaa uh iniw aya'aa.* Redictated portion: *mii ngiw oshki'aya'aansag.*

["weweni, weweni" bimi-nanaginaawaad i'iw.]
  The editors changed what sounds like *nanaginaawaawaad* to *nanaginaawaad.*

Paragraph 7

[Nibiikaang igaye,]
  Deleted duplicate: *Nibiikaang igaye.*

Ziigwan, Niibin, Dagwaagin, Biboon
Spring, Summer, Fall, Winter (Version 1)

Paragraph 1

[Anooj gii-izhichigewag ayi'ii ge]
   What sounds to be *ayi'iin geg* was clarified in redictation as
   ayi'ii gaye.

Paragraph 2

[ingikendanziin, mashkiki]
   False start deleted: *gii-mashkikii . . .*

[Gii-abinoojiinyiwiyaang, gaawiin wiikaa ingii-izhaasiimin
mashkikiiwinini.]
   Dorothy clarified and restructured this sentence and the
   preceding sentence in redictation. The original audio appeared
   as *Gaawiin awiiya mashkikiiwininiwan gii-izhaasiiwag ngii-
   izhaasiimin gii-abinoojiinyiwiyaang gaye.*

Paragraph 3

[wiiyaas, agwajiing baasamowaad,]
   False start deleted: *wiigwaas, I mean wiiyaas.*

Paragraph 4

[Anooj ige gii-pabaa-izhi-goziwag oodi-ko ge ingii-izhaamin,]
   False start deleted: *ingii-paa.*

Paragraph 5

[Dibi-go keyaa izhaawaagwen aaniindi-go onizhishininig
manoomin]
   waa- in what appears to sound like *waa-izhaagwen* is deleted in
   redictation. *Aaniindi-go* was added in redictation.

[Mii-go idi endazhi-giizhitoowaad i'iw. Gaawiin dash geyaabi izhichigesiiwag i'iw. Odayaanaawaa iw ayaabajitoowaad. Mii-ko gaa-izhichigewaad iw wiinawaa-go ogii-kiizhiitoonaawaa, mimigoshkamowaad igaye.]

This passage was revised in redictation. It had been *Mii ayaamowaad i'iw. Ogii-michi-giizhitoonaawaa-ko ngiw anishinaabeg, wiinawaa ge mimigoshkamoog naa gaye, gidasigewaad igaye.*

Paragraph 6

[gii-na'inamowaad]
gii-atoowaad was changed to *gii-na'inamowaad* in redictation.

[Mii-sh i'iw anooj gegoo gii-izhichigewag. Ogii-ozhi'aawaan iniw odaagiman.]

Original passage *Mii-sh anooj idash izhichigewag, ayi'iin ige odoozhi'aawaan ayi'iin, odaaganan* was changed in redictation to the current text. Note that *odaaganan* was changed to *odaagiman* in redictation.

Ziigwan, Niibin, Dagwaagin, Biboon
Spring, Summer, Fall, Winter (Version 2)

Paragraph 1

[Ayigwa ziigwan. Mii azhigwa zaagibagaag.]
Zhigwa added in redictation. Deleted: *iw.*

Paragraph 2

[Bineshiiwigamigoonsan igaye, miinawaa iniw makakoonsan adaawaageyaang.]

What sounded to be *Miinawaa zhigwa onaagad* was deleted. Dorothy did not repeat this portion in redictation.

[jiimaanensan igaye miinawaa wiigwaasi-jiimaanan.]
jiimaanens miinawaa wiigwaasi-jiimaan added in redictation.

Paragraph 3

[Akina gegoo ogii-paasaanaawaa na'inamowaad editemagak.]
   Past tense *gii-* and *na'inamowaad* added in redictation.

[ingoji ba-izhi-goziwaad]
   False start deleted: *babaa.*

[gii-kidasamowaad igaye.]
   False start deleted: *gii-kidasam.*

[Mii miinawaa nooshkaachigewaad]
   False start deleted: *nooshkaach.*

[mii iniw gaa-aabajitoowaad iniw nooshkaachinaaganan,]
   Dorothy changed what sounds like *gaa-aabajitoowaajin* to *gaa-aabajitoowaad iniw* in redictation.

Paragraph 4

[akawe zagaswe'idiwag.]
   bagijigewag changed to *zagaswe'idiwag* in redictation.

Paragraph 5

[Akawe da-zagaswe'idiwag waa-miijiwaad i'iw manoomin miinawaa iniw miinan oshki-miijiwaad.]
   Dorothy added this sentence in redictation.

[Mii gaa-izhichigewaad iko, asemaan asaawaad.]
   Dorothy added this sentence in redictation.

Paragraph 6

[Mii-sh iw giizhitoowaad]
   Dorothy said that she meant to say "they finish it," not "cook it." *giizizamowaad* replaced with *giizhitoowaad.*

Paragraph 9

[Gii-onizhishinini gaa-miijiwaad.]
    False start deleted: *Gaawiin.*

[Mewinzha-sh gaawiin gii-izhiwebasinoon i'iw.]
    False start deleted: first *gaawiin.*

Iskigamizigeng
Boiling Sap

Paragraph 6

[Gii-ozhiga'igewaad, maawanjitoowaad]
    False start deleted: *gaa- i'iw.*

[Gaawiin ige, gimiwaninig igaye, ezhi-ziigwebinamaang.]
    False start deleted: *gaawiin iw nibi.*

Paragraph 13

[gegoo odoozhitoonaawaa.]
    False start deleted: *odaabajitoonaawaa.*

Paragraph 14

[Ini-nitaawigiwaad igo mii ge wiinawaa miinawaa ani-izhichigewaad igo mii go miinawaa da-aabajitoowaad iniw ayi'iin iw.]
    What sounds like *wiigwaasadini* has been deleted. The consultant could not determine what this word was.

Ji-bagijiged O-miigaazod
To Make an Offering When He Goes to War

Paragraph 1

[Miinawaa bangii omaa gegoo ji-ikidoyaan iidog, asemaa
ji-dazhimag.]
    False start deleted: *Mii-sh*. Redictation: *Miinawaa gegoo
ji-ikidoyaan asemaa ji-dazhimag.*

[Gabe-ayi'ii]
    False start deleted: *Gaawiin igo.*

[Azhigwa ba-izhi-gikendamaan a'aw asemaa, omaa
inga-dibaajim.]
    Redictation: *Ezhi-gikendamaan a'aw asemaa nga-dibaajim.*

Paragraph 2

[Omaa gii-maajaawaad ongow indawemaag o-miigaazowaad]
    Redictation: *Gii-maajaawaad ingiw indinawemaaganag
gii-o-miigaazowaad.*

[Mii-sh imaa endaayaang nimaamaa endaad, niibowa omaa, mii
imaa ingiw onji-maajaawaad ingiw gwiiwizensag Gwiiwizensiwi-
ziibiing imaa akina gii-ayaawaad.]
    Redictation: *Mii imaa gaa-onji-maajaawaad ngiw niibowa
gwiiwizensag Gwiiwizensiwiziibiing, imaa kina gii-ayaawaad.
Mii imaa gaa-onji-maajaawaad.*

Paragraph 3

[Mii-sh imaa nimindimooyenyag imaa gii-ayaawaad,]
    Redictation: *Mii-sh imaa mindimooyenyag imaa gii-ayaawag.*
What sounds like *aw* before *mindimooyenyag* is deleted.

["Gego, gego nibiikaang miigaazokegon.]
    Redictation: *Gego imaa nibiikaang dazhi-miigaazokegon.*

Paragraph 5

[ingiw]
    ngiw inserted in redictation.

[Gaawiin igo awiiya ingikenimaasiin imaa gaa-gikenimag
gii-aapidendid.]
    Redictation: *Gaawiin awiiya imaa ngikenimaasiin awiiya
    ji-gii-aapidendid.*

Paragraph 6

[Chi-mookomaan ogii-ozhi'aan iniw asemaan.]
    Redictation: *Chi-mookomaanag ngiw ogii-ozhi'aawaan iniw
    asemaan.*

[ingichi-anishinaabemag.]
    Redictation: *ngiw ngichi-anishinaabemag.*

Paragraph 7

[Bijiinag-sh igo ge wiinawaa asemaa.]
    Redictation: *Bijiinag dash igo i'iw gaye wiinawaa iniw asemaan.*

Agoodwewin
Snaring

Paragraph 3

[Aw nishiime, iwidi ge wiin bakaan dazhi-agoodoo.]
    Original sentence in audio replaced with redictated sentence.

[Ayaa idi waabamag biijibatood mii gaa-pi-baabiibaagid.]
    Original sentence in audio replaced with redictated sentence.

Gii-pi-bajiishka'ondwaa
When They Came to Give Them Shots

Paragraph 2

[Gii-maajiizhiyangid]
    The editors wrote what sounds like *maajii'iyangid* as
maajiizhiyangid.

Paragraph 3

[Nimaamaa chi-gaaskanazootawag, "Maam, mii-na gii-niboyan?"
"Gaawiin," ikido.]
    False start deleted: *Nimaamaanaan.*

Gii-twaashin Mikwamiing
He Fell through the Ice

Paragraph 1

[Agaami-zaaga'igan iwidi, gii-piboon idash, gii-ayaamagad idi *a
logging camp.*]
    False start deleted: *endazhi-giiwash . . .*

[Bangii-go imaa indebaabamaanaanig]
    What sounds like *debaabamid* is replaced by
indebaabamaanaanig as suggested by one of our consultants.

Shut Up!

Paragraph 3

[Gaawiin gegoo ingii-pizindanziimin.]
    False start deleted: *gegoo.*

[Dagoshing ganawaabamangid chi-mookomaanikwens imaa
biindiged—chi-mookomaanikwe.]
    False start deleted: *moonik.*

Paragraph 4

[Gwaakwaashkwaniyaang]
    False start deleted: what sounds like *i'iw*.

Paragraph 5

[Meta-go gii-ojibwemoyaang.]
    False start deleted: *Gaawiin*.

Bagida'waang Zaaga'iganiing
Fishing with a Net on a Lake

Paragraph 1

[Mezinaashiikwe indizhinikaaz.]
    English deleted: *Dorothy Whipple, people call me. My real name is Dora Whipple Mitchell, from the Mitchells up there.*

[Mii-sh i'iw egooyaan omaa ji-dibaajimoyaan o'ow bagida'waawin, ji-dazhindamaan.]
    Mii-sh i'iw egooyaan ji-dibaajimoyaan o'ow bagida'wing, bagida'waawin ji-dazhindamaan changed in redictation. *ngiw* deleted in redictation.

Paragraph 2

[Gii-gichi-anokiiwag-sago.]
    -sago was added in redictation.

[Gaye niin ingii-izhichige.]
    What sounds like *ngii-izhichige-sago gaye niin igo* was changed in redictation.

[Noongom bagida'waawaad,]
    Noongom was added in redictation.

106

Paragraph 3

[Waawanoonsan igaye gii-kiizizang iko nimaamaa.]
   Ige was deleted in redictation.

Paragraph 5

[Gaye niin-sh igo azhigwa netaawigiyaan, ayi'iing-ko
ingii-pagida'waa]
   Dorothy redictated: *Gaye niin dash ayigwa netaawigiyaan,*
   ayi'iing-ko ngii-pagida'waa.

[Chi-neniibowa iko ingii-pagida'waamin.]
   What sounds like *ngiw* in the final position was deleted.

[Chi-mookomaan asabiig idash ingii-aabaji'aanaanig.]
   Sentence clarified in redictation. What sounds like *niinawind*
   ayigwa was deleted in redictation.

Wii-maji-doodawaad Awiiya A'aw Gookooko'oo
When the Owl Treated Someone Bad

Paragraph 5

[Onzaam ingii-abinoojiinyiwimin, gaawiin ingii-
waabanda'igoosiimin a'aw gookooko'oo gaa-nisinjin.]
   False start deleted: *Gaawiin dash.*

Agoodweng Waaboozoon
Snaring a Rabbit

Paragraph 2

[Iko gii-abinoojiinyiwiyaang, ingii-kii'igoshimigoomin.]
   False start deleted: *ingii- uh ingii-kii'igoshimigoomin.*

Paragraph 3

[Chi-gigizheb]
    False start deleted: *Gigizheb.*

[Gii'igoshimoyaang iko,]
    iko was added in redictation.

Paragraph 4

[Iw gabe-giizhik babaa-ayaayaang megwaayaak, aw nishiime
anooj igo nishiimeyag miinawaa cousins.]
    In redictation, Dorothy stated that her nephews were with her,
    too; she never said this in the Ojibwe portion of the story, but
    we included it in the English translation.

Paragraph 5

[Aanish naa ingii-maazhichigemin iw gii-izhichigeyaang.]
    In redictation, Dorothy said *ingii-maazhichigemin-sago
    gii-izhichigeyaang.*

Manoominike-zaaga'igan
Rice Lake

Paragraph 1

[Ayi'iing iko idi ingii-taamin]
    Redictation: *Ayi'iing iko iwidi nigii-taamin.*

Paragraph 2

[Ayi'iing-sh iko idi ingii-o-manoominikemin,]
    Redictation: *Mii-sh-ko iwidi ngii-o-manoominikemin.*

[Gaawiin awiiya imaa bakaan gii-piindiganaasiin
ji-manoominiked.]
    Redictation: *Gaawiin imaa awiiya daa-biindiganaasiin
    ji-manoominiked.*

108

Paragraph 4

[gaa-izhaayaang o-manoominikeyaang.]
  Redictation: *gii-o-manoominikeyaang.*

[Mii-sh iwidi ingoding]
  Hard to understand the original audio; clarified in redictation.

[megwaayaak keyaa gii-pi-izhaadog.]
  Redictation: *gii-pi-izhaawag.*

[Ayi'iin ige iw, wiinizisimaanan ogii-piizikaanaawaan.]
  In the original recording, *owiinizisimaanan* (with an initial /o/)
  can be heard. The second time Dorothy uses this word in the
  recording, it's without the initial /o/. In redictation, an initial
  /o/ isn't heard. Therefore, *wiinizisimaanan* is used here instead
  of *owiinizisimaanan* as it seems to be in the recording. In
  redictation, Dorothy offered a few sentences, both without initial
  /o/: (a) *Miinawaa wiinizisimaanan ogii-piizikaanaawaan.* (b)
  Miinawaa ogii-piizikaanaawaan iniw wiinizisimaanan.

Paragraph 5

[babaa-ayaawag]
  Redictation: *gii-pabaa-ayaawag.*

Paragraph 6

[Mii-sh i'iw gaa-izhi-waabamaawaad iniw,]
  Redictation: *Mii dash i'iw gaa-izhi-waabamaawaad iniw, . . .*

[Niizh iniw]
  ngiw changed to *iniw* in redictation.

Gii-maazhendam Gii-nanawizid
He Was Upset When He Was Empty-Handed

Paragraph 1

[Omaa akawe gegoo inga-dibaajim gaa-izhiwebak iko.]
Aansh omaa nga-dibaajim gegoo gaa-izhiwebak iko changed in redictation.

[Iwidi ingii-taamin iko idi ayi'iing, Remer idi.]
In redictation: *Iwidi-ko ngii-taamin iwidi Remer iwidi.*

[Aya'aa ogii-nooji'aan iniw aya'aan zhaangweshiwan.]
Deleted: *a mink, a mink.* In redictation, Dorothy provided the unobviated form *zhaangweshi* for *mink.* The obviated form *zhaangweshiwan* was provided here by the editors; it was also checked and approved by the consultants. This usage is consistent with Dorothy's use of the obviative form *zhaangweshiwan* in other parts of the story.

Paragraph 2

[mink iniw zhaangweshiwan.]
Deleted: *gii-ayaad.* The editors provided the obviated form *zhaangweshiwan.*

[Mii-sh i'iw gii-maajiinaawaad]
mii-sh igo replaced with *mii-sh i'iw* in redictation.

Paragraph 3

[Mii-sh a'aw inini imaa ezhi-atood wanii'igaans.]
Azhigwa besho imaa ayaanid iniw, gikenimaad ayaanid, miigid, mii-sa inini imaa wanii'igan imaa ezhi-atood deleted and replaced in redictation.

110

Paragraph 4

[Aanind wiin igo ogii-tebibinaawaan igo, wiikobinaawaad imaa waanikaaning.]
Deleted in redictation: *a hole.*

Paragraph 5

[Mii-sh azhigwa iko]
ayigwa replaced with *azhigwa* in redictation.

[Mii i'iw gii-mikawaawaad]
Mii ii changed to *mii i'iw* in redictation. Dorothy said in redictation: *mii i'iw gii-nisaawaad.*

[Mii i'iw azhigwa gawishimod.]
In redictation, Dorothy says what sounds like *Mii iw maazhendang mii i'iw zhigwa gawishimod, mii gii-nanawiziwaad.*

Ogii-miigaadaanaawaa I'iw Waazakonenjigan Imaa Atood Miinawaa Iw Aazhogan
They Fought to Have That Stoplight and Bridge Put In

Paragraph 1

[Aanish niwii-tazhindaan imaa iw, imaa ayi'iing *Little Earth 1973* imaa *I've been living there.*]
False start deleted: *I was one of the . . .*

[gii-niiwanishkooziwag.]
See also *niiwanishkoozo.*

[gii-bizikooziwag]
See also *bizikoozo.*

[imaa ingiw]
aw replaced with *ingiw* as suggested by Johnny Mitchell. Other

111

places where *aw* is used to denote plurality are also replaced with *ingiw* for grammatical purposes.

Paragraph 2

[Mii a'aw gaa-atood imaa i'iw waazakonenjiganan.]
  False start deleted: *I remember, I don't know.*

[weweni imaa aazhawishkaayaan imaa.]
  Johnny Mitchell suggested that the last word should be *imaa.*

Paragraph 4

[Geget igo, anooj igo awiiya geget iw, geget baataniinowag ingiw.]
  Johnny Mitchell added *awiiya* and *ingiw.*

Paragraph 6

[Weweni inganawenimigoomin igaye gii-achigaadeg gegoo dekaag igaye.]
  False start deleted: *Weweni inganawenimigoomin imaa.*

Imbiindaakoojige Imaa Asiniing
I Made an Offering There on the Rock

Paragraph 2

[gii-izhaayaan gii-o-waabamag]
  -o- added to *gii-waabamag* in redictation.

[Mii idi gaa-izhaayaan chi-waasa.]
  chi-waasa added in redictation.

[Ingii-segiz imaa mayaajaayaan.]
  What sounds to be *i'iw* is replaced with *imaa* in redictation.

[Sa-ingii-minwendam gii-o-waabamag aw noozhishenh.]
  False start that sounds to be *Aansh gaawiin* deleted.
  Original sentence, which sounds to be *Shago gaawiin*

niminwendam-sago di-gii-waabamag noozhishenh, is replaced with redictated statement.

Paragraph 3

[Mii-sh iwidi, gii-ni-ayaayaang idi Colorado.]
ayi'iing ngii-ayaamin replaced with redictated portion.

[asemaa wii-o-asag.]
-o- added in redictation.

[Mii-sh igo gii-mikwenimagwaa ingiw.]
What sounds like *mii-sh iw maamiikwenimagwa* is changed to *mii-sh igo gii-mikwenimagwaa* in redictation. *i-gaa-inendamaan* was deleted in redictation.

[Miziwe gigii-ayaamin omaa akiing.]
False start deleted: *o'ow.* Redictated sentence: *Miziwe ge wiinawaa omaa gii-ayaawaagwen omaa akiing* ("They probably stay in that land").

Paragraph 4

[Mii-go ezhi-bimiwinag aw asemaa.]
-go added in redictation.

Paragraph 6

[Chi-mewinzha iko ge wiin gichi-anishinaabeg gii-tazhimaawaad iko asemaan.]
Shortened in redictation and replaced the original phrasing: *Chi-mewinzh ngichi-anishinaabeg gaye niin chi-mewinzha-ko ngichi-anishinaabemag gii-kaagiigidowaad, apane asemaan gii-tazhimaawaad.*

[Meta-go wii-sagaswaanaawaad asemaan.]
The editors changed what is heard as *ayaangwaam* or *ayaangwaamaad* to *Meta-go wii-sagaswaanaawaad asemaan.* One of the consultants suggested that it might be *Meta-go*

113

ayaangwaamiziwaad wii-sagaswaanaawaad asemaan for the meaning "All they wanted to do was smoke." Another consultant suggested *Meta-go wii-sagaswaanaawaad asemaan.*

Makwa Ingii-pimaaji'ig
Bear Saved My Life

Paragraph 1

[Gaye-sh idi gaawiin-go weweni nimino-bimosesiin.]
What appears to be *eta-go bimoseyaan wayiimaa aanch* was deleted. The consultant was not able to determine what Dorothy was saying here, so it was treated as a false start and left out of the text.

Paragraph 2

[Niibowa ogikenimaan igo iniw anishinaaben medewinijin miinawaa iniw nenaandawi'iwenijin.]
The editors changed what sounds like *nanenaandawi'iwenijin* to *iniw nenaandawi'iwenijin.* This seems to fit the pattern just before when Dorothy said *iniw anishinaaben medewinijin.*

[Aaniish naa ingii-kagiibishe.]
The editors deleted *-yaan* in *ingii-kagiibisheyaan.*

Paragraph 4

[Niin niwii-miigaanig.]
False start deleted: *gagwe niin niwii-k . . .*

[Gegoo niwii-toodaag]
The editors changed what sounds to be *gegoo niwii-taadaag* to *gegoo niwii-toodaag* as no redictation was available for this portion of the story.

Glossary

Grammatical Codes

adv	adverb
adv conj	conjunctive adverb
adv deg	degree adverb
adv gram	grammatical adverb
adv loc	locational adverb
adv man	manner adverb
adv num	number adverb
adv pred	predicate adverb
adv qnt	quantitative adverb
adv tmp	temporal adverb
na	animate noun
na-v	animate participle
nad	dependent animate noun
name place	place name
ni	inanimate noun
nid	dependent inanimate noun
pc disc	discourse particle
pron dem	demonstrative pronoun
pron psl	pausal pronoun
pv dir	directional preverb
pv lex	lexical preverb
pv rel	relative preverb
pv tns	tense/mode preverb
vai	animate intransitive verb
vai + o	animate intransitive verb with object
vii	inanimate intransitive verb

voc	vocative
vta	transitive animate verb
vti	transitive inanimate verb (e.g., *mikan*, find it)
vti2	class 2 transitive inanimate verb (e.g., *biidoon*, bring it)
vti3	class 3 transitive inanimate verb (e.g., *miijin*, eat it)
vti4	class 4 transitive inanimate verb

---

aanish *adv man* well, well now
abinoojiinh, abinoojiinyag *na* child
abinoojiinyiwi *vai* s/he is a child
abwe *vai + o* s/he roasts or cooks over a fire
abwiins, -an *ni* little paddle
achigaade *vii* it is put there, it is placed there, they put/place it there
aditemagad *vii* it is ripe
adaawaage *vai + o* s/he sells
adaawam *vta* borrow it from him/her
adik, -wag *na* caribou, reindeer
adim *vta* catch up to him/her, overtake him/her
agaami-zaaga'igan *adv loc* across the lake
agaasaa *vii* it is small
agaashiinyi *vai* s/he is small

115

agaawaa *adv deg* barely

agwanji'onaagan, -an *ni* float for a net

agoodaw *vta* set a snare for him/her

agoodoo *vai* s/he sets a snare (also, **agoodwe**)

agoodwe *vai* s/he sets a snare (also, **agoodoo**)

agoozh /agooN-/ *vta* hang him/her

agwajiing *adv loc* outside

akakanzhe *ni* coals or charcoal

akamaw *vta* lie in wait for him/her

aki, -n *ni* earth, ground, land

akik, -oog *na* pail, kettle, pot

akiwenzii, -yag *na* old man

andawaabam *vta* look for him/her (see also **nandawaabam**)

ani- *pv dir* on the way, becoming, as it happens

aniibiishibag, -oon *ni* leaf

animikii -g *na* thunderbird

animoons, -ag *na* puppy

animoonzhish *na* poor puppy

animosh, -ag *na* dog

anishinaabe, -g *na* Indian person, an Indian

anishinaabens, -sag *na* a little Indian person

anishinaabewi *vai* s/he is an Indian

anokaadan *vti* work on it

anokii *vai* s/he works

apagidoon *vti2* throw it

apakwaan, -an *ni* roof

apiichi- *pv rel* extent, to what extent

apiichigamide *vii* how much it is cooked, boils

apishimon, -an *ni* rug

asab, -iig *na* net

asemaa *na* tobacco

ashange *vai* s/he feeds people, serves food

ashi-niiwi *vai* be fourteen

ashi /aS-/ *vta* put him/her there

asin, -iig *na* stone, stones

ataage-mashkiki *ni* medicine for gambling, gambling medicine

atoon *vti* put it there

awensiinh, awensiinyag *na* wild animal

awibaa *vii* it is calm, it is a clear day

aya'aa *pron psl* what's-his-name, what's-her-name

ayaa *vai* s/he exists, there is (animate)

ayaamagad *vii* it exists, there is (inanimate)

ayaan *vti4* have it

ayaaw *vta* have him/her

ayigwa *adv tmp* now

azhegiiwe *vai* s/he returns home

azhewizh /azhewiN-/ *vta* take him/her back

aabaji' *vta* use him/her

aabajichigan, -an *ni* tool

aabajitoon *vti2* use it

aabawaa *vii* it is warm or mild weather

aabita *adv num* half

aagim, -ag *na* snowshoe

aakozi *vai* s/he is sick

aanakwad, -oon *ni* cloud

aano- *pv* in vain, try to (but for some reason cannot)

aapidendi *vai* s/he goes and does not return

aawi *vai* s/he is a certain thing or being

aazhawishkaa *vai* s/he crosses the street

aazhogan, -an *ni* bridge

babaamenim *vta* bother with him/her

babaamose *vai* s/he walks about

bagamibizo *vai* s/he arrives driving

bagida'waa *vai* s/he fishes with a net, sets a net

bagidin *vta* allow him/her

bagijige *vai* s/he makes an offering

bajiishka' /bajiishka'W/ *vta* give him/her a shot of medicine

bakaan *adv man* different

bakwan *vii* it peels off

bakwezhigan, -ag *na* bread

bami'idizo *vai* s/he supports herself/himself

bashkwegin-omakizin, -an *ni* hide moccasin

bawa'am *vai* s/he knocks or harvests wild rice

baa- *pv dir* around, about

baabiibaagi *vai* s/he keeps calling out, shouting, hollering

baaga' /baaga'W-/ *vta* pound on him/her

baaka'aakwenh, baaka'aakwenyag *na* chicken

baakaakosin *vii* it is open

baakin *vta* open him/her up

baapaase -g *na* woodpecker

baapi *vai* s/he laughs

baapinakamigizi *vai* s/he is excited

baas /baasW-/ *vta* dry him/her

baasan *vti* dry it

baashkikwa'am *vai2* s/he makes loud claps of thunder (referring to the thunderbirds) (also **baashkakwa'am**)

baashkiz /baashkizW-/ *vta* shoot him/her

baataniino *vai* be plenty, be many, be much

baazhizikaw *vta* go right over him/her

babaa- *pv dir* going about here and there

bebakaan *adv man* all different, each different one

bebezhigooganzhii, -iig *na* horse

bi- *pv dir* come to, come and

bi-azhegiiwe *vai* s/he comes back

bi-waaban *vii* dawn approaches

biboon *vii* it is winter

biboonagizi *vai* s/he is a certain number of winters old

bimaadizi *vai* s/he lives, is alive

bimaaji' *vta* save his/her life, spare him/her

bimi- *pv dir* pass by

bimi-ayaa *vai* s/he goes along, travels along

bimi-gaagiigido *vai* talking along the way

bimi-zhawenim *vta* have compassion on him/her while going by

bimibizo *vai* s/he drives along

biminizha' /biminizha'W/ *vta* chase him/her along

bimise *vai* s/he flies along

bimiwizh /bimiwiN-/ *vta* carry him/her along, take him/her along

bimoondan *vti* carry it along on your back

bimose *vai* s/he walks along, walks by

bineshiiwigamigoons, -an *ni* birdhouse

bizhishig *adv* only, empty, nothing but

bizikoozh /bizikooN/ *vta* run him/her over, strike him/her with a car

bizikoozo *vai* s/he is hit by a car

bizindan *vti* listen to it

bizindaw *vta* listen to him/her

biibaagim *vta* call out, shout, holler to him/her

biibiiwi *vai* s/he is a baby

biidoon *vti* bring it

biidwewidam *vai* s/he comes making noise

biijibatoo *vai* s/he runs here

biina'an *vti* put it in

biinakamigaa *vii* it is clean ground

biindaakoojige *vai* s/he makes an offering

biindigegozi *vai* s/he moves in

biindigazh /biindigaN-/ *vta* bring him/her inside, take him/her inside

biini' *vta* clean him/her

biiwaabikoons, -an *ni* wire

biizikan *vti* wear it

boodawe *vai* s/he builds a fire

117

bookoshkan *vti* break it in two with your foot or body

boopoodaajige *vai* snarling (literally, continually blowing air in and out)

boozi *vai* s/he gets into a vehicle, rides

chi- *pv lex* great, big

chi-anishinaabe, -g *na* an elder

chi-anokiiwin *ni* hard work

chi-aya'aa, -g *na* elder

chi-aya'aawi *vai* s/he is an elder (see also **gichi-aya'aawi**)

chi-gigizheb *adv tmp* really early (in the morning)

chi-mamaandido *vai* s/he is really big

chi-mewinzha *adv tmp* a really long time ago

chi-mewinzhakamig *adv tmp* a really long time ago

chi-mookomaan, -ag *na* white person (literally, big knife)

chi-mookomaanenzhish, -ag *na (pejorative)* naughty little white kid, that old white person

chi-mookomaanikwe, -g *na* white woman

chi-mookomaanikwens, -ag *na* little white woman

chi-neniibowa *adv qnt* a whole lot of each

chi-ozaagaskwaajime, -g *na* a big leech

chi-waasa *adv loc* really far away

dadazhindan *vti* continually talk about it, discuss it

dagoshin *vai* s/he arrives

dagwaagin *vii* it is fall

dakobizh /dakobiN-/ *vta* tie him/her, bind him/her

dakoniwewinini, -wag *na* game warden, police officer

dashi *vai* s/he is a certain number (usually said in the plural)

dasogon *adv num* so many days

dazhi- *pv rel* there, place where

dazhim *vta* talk about him/her

dazhindan *vti* talk about it

daa *vai* s/he lives there

debaabam *vta* have him/her in sight, see him/her from a distance

debaabandan *vti* have it in sight, see it from a distance

debibizh /debibiN-/ *vta* grab him/her, catch him/her

debwe *vai* s/he tells the truth

debweyendam *vai* s/he believes

dekaag *ni-v* ice cream (changed form of **dakaa,** be cold)

dewe'igaans, -ag *na* little drum

diba' /diba'W/ *vta* pay for him/her

dibaajim *vta* tell about him/her

dibaajimo *vai* s/he tells a story, narrates

doodaazo *vai* s/he does something to herself/himself

doodaw *vta* do it to him/her

doodooshaaboo-bimide *ni* butter

dwaashin *vai* s/he falls through the ice

enda- *pv lex* really

endaso-dibik *adv tmp* every night

endaso-giizhigak *ni-v* every day (also **endaso-giizhik**)

endazhi- *pv rel* place where (changed form of **dazhi-**)

endazhigidaazod *na-v* where s/he is angry (changed form of **dazhigidaazo**)

endaad *na-v* where s/he lives, her/his house (changed form of **daa**)

endaawaad *na-v* where they live, their house (changed form of **daa**)

endaayaang *na-v* where we live (exclusive), our house (exclusive) (changed form of **daa**)

eniwek *pv man* kind of, somewhat, quite

ezhi- *pv rel* in what manner, and then, and so

ga- *pv tns* (future tense marker)

gabe-biboon *adv tmp* all winter

gabe-giizhik *adv tmp* all day

gabe-niibin *adv tmp* all summer

gaganawaabam *vta* keep looking at him/her

gaganoozh /gaganooN-/ *vta* speak to him/her

gagiibaadizi *vai* s/he is crazy

gagiibishe *vai* s/he is deaf

gagwejim *vta* ask him/her

ganawaabam *vta* look at him/her

ganawendan *vti* take care of it

ganawenim *vta* take care of him/her

ganawenjigaade *vii* it is taken care of, they take care of it

gashki' *vta* be able to get him/her to

gashkitoon *vti2* be able to do it

gawishimo *vai* s/he lies down, goes to bed

Gaa-zagaskwaajimekaag *name place* Leech Lake Reservation

gaagiigido *vai* s/he speaks

gaagiimaabam *vta* keep spying on him/her

gaaskanazootaw *vta* whisper to him/her

gaazh /gaaN-/ *vta* hide him/her

gezikwendan *vti* vaguely remember it

gibwanaabaawe *vai* s/he drowns

gichi-anishinaabe, -g *na* an elder

gichi-anokii *vai* s/he really works

gichi-awan *vii* it is really foggy

gichi-aya'aawi *vai* s/he is an elder (see also **chi-aya'aawi**)

gichi-odaabaan -ag *na* big vehicle

gichi-waasa *adv loc* really far away

gidasan *vti* parch it

gijiiigibizh /gijiiigibiN-/ *vta* skin him/her (especially animals)

gikaa *vai* s/he is elderly, is old

gikendan *vti* know it

gikenim *vta* know him/her

gikinoo'amaadiiwigamig, -oon *ni* school

gikinoo'amaw *vta* teach him/her

gimiwan *vii* it is raining

ginjiba' *vta* run away from him/her

gitigaan, -an *ni* garden, farm

gizhaate *vii* it is hot (outside)

gizhiibide *vii* it moves fast, flies fast, speeds fast

gii- *pv tns* (past tense marker)

gii'igoshimo *vai* s/he fasts for a vision

giigoonh, giigoonyag *na* fish

giikaji *vai* s/he is cold

giishka'aakwe *vai* s/he cuts timber

giishpin *adv gram* if

giiwashkwebii *vai* s/he is drunk

giiwe *vai* s/he goes home

giiwenh *pc disc* so the story goes, so it is said, apparently

giiwewizh /giiwewiN-/ *vta* take him/her home, carry him/her home

giiyose *vai* s/he hunts

giizhide *vii* it is hot

giizhigin *vii* it is ripe

giizhiitaa *vai* s/he finishes a task, work

giizhiikan *vti* finish it

giizhikaandag, -oog *na* cedar bough

giizhitoon *vti2* finish it, finish making it

giizhoozhi *vai* s/he keeps warm

giiziz /giizizW-/ *vta* finish cooking him/her

giizizan *vti* finish cooking it

-go *pc disc* an emphatic word (full form: **igo**)

goshi /goS-/ *vta* fear him/her!

119

gotan *vti* fear it

gozi *vai* s/he moves her/his residence

gookooko'oo, -g *na* owl

goon *na* snow

gwayakochige *vai* s/he makes things right, does things right

gwaakwaashkwani *vai* s/he jumps up and down

gwiiwizens, -ag *na* boy

Gwiiwizensiwi-zaaga'iganiing *name place* Boy Lake

Gwiiwizensiwi-ziibiing *name place* Boy River

ige *adv conj* also (also **igaye**)

i'iw *pron dem* that, that one, the

ikido *vai* s/he says

ikonaazha' /ikonaazha'W-/ *vta* drive him/her off

ikwe, -wag *na* woman

ikwezens, -ag *na* little girl

imaa *adv loc* there

imbaabaa *nad* my father

inaabadizi *vai* s/he is used in a certain way

inaabi *vai* s/he peeks, looks there

inaajimo *vai* s/he tells it that way, narrates a certain way

inaapine *vai* s/he is sick with some type of illness

inakamigad *vii* it happens a certain way

inawem *vta* be related to him/her

inawemaagan, -ag *na* a relative

indaanis, -ag *nad* my daughter

indawemaa, -g *nad* my sibling of the opposite sex

inendan *vti* think of it a certain way

ingoding *adv tmp* sometime, one time, at one time, sometime later

ingoji *adv deg* somewhere, approximately, about

ingwana *pc disc* it turns out that

inigaa' *vta* be mean to him/her, injure him/her

inigini *vai* s/he is so big, a certain size

inini, -wag *na* man

iniw *pron dem* those (inanimate)

iniw *pron dem* that, those (obviative)

inzhishenh, inzhishenyag *nad* my uncle (mother's brother)

ishkwaa- *pv asp* stop, done

ishkweyaang *adv loc* behind

ishpaginzo *vai* s/he is worth a lot of money, high-priced, expensive

ishpatemagad *vii* the snow is high

iskigamizigan, -an *ni* a sugar bush, a sugar camp

iskigamizige *vai* s/he boils sap down

iwidi *adv loc* (or *idi*) over there

izhaa *vai* s/he goes to a certain place, goes there

izhi- *pv rel* in a certain manner, and then, and so

izhi' *vta* do with him/her in a certain manner

izhi /iN-/ *vta* say it to him/her

izhichige *vai* s/he does things

izhinaazhikaw *vta* chase him/her to a certain place

izhinikaadan *vti* name it a certain way, call it that way

izhinikaade *vii* it is named so, they call it such

izhinikaazh /izhinikaaN-/ *vta* name, call him/her that

izhinikaazo *vai* s/he is named so, they call her/him that

izhinizha' *vta* /izhinizha'W/ send him/her to a certain place

izhiwebad *vii* it happens a certain way, how it happens

izhiwebizi *vai* s/he fares a certain way, s/he has something happen to him/her, something is wrong with him/her

izhiwizh /izhiwiN-/ *vta* take him/her to a certain place

jaagizan *vti* burn it up

ji- *pv tns* to, in order to, so that

jibwaa- *pv tns* before

jiibaakwe *vai* s/he cooks

jiigi- *pv lex* next to

jiigibiig *adv loc* next to the water

jiimaanens, -an *ni* little boat

jiime *vai* s/he paddles, canoes

jiisakii *vai* s/he uses a shaking tent

maji- *pv lex* bad, evil

maji-aya'aawish *na* an evil person

maji-mashkiki *ni* bad medicine, poison

maji-doodaw *vta* treat him/her in an evil way

makadewizi *vai* s/he is black in color

makakoons, -an *ni* little box

makwa, -g *na* bear

mami /mam-/ *vta* take him/her, pick him/her up

mamoon *vti* take it, pick it up

manidoo, -g *na* spirit

manidoowendam *vai* s/he has sacred feelings for something, thinks sacredly

manoomin *ni* wild rice

manoominike *vai* s/he harvests wild rice

Manoominike-zaaga'igan *name place* Rice Lake

mashkawaakwaji *vai* s/he is frozen stiff

mashkawaakwajim *vta* freeze him/her

mashkawizii *vai* s/he is strong, powerful

mashkiki, -wan *ni* medicine

mashkikiikaazh /mashkikiikaaN-/ *vta* doctor him/her

mashkikiiwinini, -wag *na* medicine man

mashkimod, -an *ni* bag

mashkode-bizhiki, -wag *na* buffalo

mawinzo *vai* s/he picks berries

mayaginaw *vta* sense something strange about him/her

mazinaakide *vii* it is pictured, photographed

maagizhaa *adv man* maybe

maajaa *vai* s/he leaves

maajiizh *vta* take him/her away, along

maajiidoon *vti2* take it along

maajitaa *vai* s/he starts an activity

maam *voc* mom

maaminonendan *vti* notice, realize it

maawanji'idiwag- *vai* they meet together, have a meeting

maawanjitoon *vti* collect it into a group

maazhendam *vai* s/he feels bad

maazhichige *vai* s/he does something bad

megwaayaak *adv loc* in the woods

midewi *vai* s/he is a member of the Midewiwin (Medicine Society)

migi *vai* s/he barks

mii *adv pred*

mikan *vti* find it

mikaw *vta* find him

mikwendam *vai* s/he remembers, comes to mind, gets an idea

mikwenim *vta* remember him/her

mimigoshkam *vai* s/he dances on wild rice, threshes wild rice

minawaanigozi *vai* s/he has fun

minawaanigwendam *vai* s/he is glad, happy

mindido *vai* s/he is big

mindimooyenh, mindimooyenyag *na* old woman

minikwe *vai + o* s/he drinks (it)

mino- *pv lex* good

mino-ayaa *vai* s/he is good, is fine

minwaabaawe *vai* s/he is well soaked

minwendam *vai* s/he is glad, happy

mitig, -oon *ni* stick, log, piece of wood

mitigo-makakoons, -an *ni* wooden container

miigaadan *vti* fight it, fight for it (a cause)

miigaadi- *vai* fight each other (usually said in the plural)

miigaazh /miigaaN-/ *vta* fight him/her

miigaazo *vai* s/he fights

miijin *vti3* eat it

miikana, -an *ni* road, trail

miin, -an *ni* blueberry

miizh /miiN-/ *vta* give it to him/her

mookii *vai* s/he emerges from the surface

mookomaan, -an *ni* knife

moonikaazh *vta* dig a hole to get him/her out

na'inan *vti* store it away

naboob *ni* soup

nagamo *vai* s/he sings

nagwaazh /nagwaaN-/ *vta* snare him/her

nakweshkaw *vta* meet him/her

namadabi *vai* s/he sits

nanagin *vta* control, hold him/her back

nanaandawi' *vta* heal, doctor him/her

nanaandawi'iwe *vai* s/he heals, doctors people

nandawaabam *vta* look for him/her, search for him/her (see also **andawaabam**)

nandom *vta* invite, call for him/her

nandone'an *vti* look for it

napodinike *vai* s/he makes dumplings

naadagwe *vai* s/he checks snares

naadasabii *vai* s/he gets nets from the water

naadin *vti3* get it, fetch it

naanaagadawendan *vti* consider it, think about it

nanawizi *vai* s/he comes back empty handed, has no luck (in a hunt)

naaniibowa *adv qnt* lots

naaningodinong *adv tmp* sometimes

naano-biboonagizi *vai* s/he is five years old

naasaab *adv man* the same

nibaagan, -an *ni* bed

nibi *ni* water

nibiikaa *vii* there is a lot of water

nibo *vai* s/he dies, is dead

nibwaakaa *vai* s/he is smart, wise

nichiiwakamagad *vii* it is a protest, a riot

nimaamaanaan *nad* grandmother

nimaamaa *nad* my mother

nimisenh *nad* my older sister

nimishoomis *nad* my grandfather

niniijaanis, -ag *nad* my child

nisayenh, nisayenyag *nad* my older brother

nishi /niS-/ *vta* kill him/her

nishigiiwanizi *vai* s/he causes a ruckus, raising hell, causing a disturbance

nishiime *nad* my younger sibling

nishkaadenim *vta* be angry at him/her

nishwanaajichige *vai* s/he wastes, destroys, spoils things

nisidawinan *vti* recognize it

nisidotam *vai* s/he understands

nisidotan *vti* understand it

nitaa- *pv lex* know how, likes to

nitaawichige *vai* s/he is skilled at things

nitaawigi *vai* s/he grows up

nitaawigi' *vta* raise him/her

nitawag, -an *nid* my ear

niibawi *vai* s/he stands
niibin *vii* it is summer
niigaanizi *vai* s/he leads, is in charge
niiwanishkoozo *vai* s/he is killed in an accident
niizho-biboonagad *vii* two years ago, two years pass
niizhogon *adv num* two days
noogishkaa *vai* s/he stops moving
noogishkaa' *vta* stop him/her from moving
nooji' *vta* hunt, go after him/her
noondaagozi *vai* s/he is heard
noondam *vai* s/he hears
noondaw *vta* hear him/her
noondese *vai* s/he runs short of things
nooshkaachinaagan, -an *ni* basket for winnowing rice
nooshkaachige *vai* s/he winnows or fans rice
noozishenh, noozishenyag *nad* my grandchild
odaabaan, -ag *na* car
odamino *vai* s/he plays
odayan *nad* his dog, horse
odoodemi *vai* s/he has a clan
ogijayi'ii *adv loc* on top of it
ojibwemo *vai* s/he speaks Ojibwe
ojibwemowin *ni* Ojibwe language
okaadakik, -oog *na* kettle with legs
okan, -an *nid* his/her bone
ombiigizi *vai* s/he is loud, is noisy
ombin *vta* lift him/her
onaagoshin *vii* it is evening
ondendi *vai* s/he is gone from a certain place
ondin *vta* get him/her from there
oniijaanisan *nad* his child/children
oninawe'an *vti* stir it

onishkaanaazha' /onishkaanizha'W/ *vta* run in there and wake him/her up
onizhishin *vii* it is nice, it is pretty
onizhishin *vai* it is good
onji- *pv rel* from where, why
onjibaa *vai* s/he is from a certain place
onzaabi *vai* s/he looks out from a certain place
onzan *vti* boil it
oodena, -wan *ni* town
opwaagan, -ag *na* pipe
oshki- *pv lex* new
oshki-aya'aans, -ag *na* young one
oshki-inini, -wag *na* young man
oshkiniigikwe, -g *na* young woman
owiijiikiwenyan *nad* his brother
ozagaskwaajime, -g *na* it a leech
ozhi' *vta* make him/her
ozhiga'ige *vai* s/he taps trees
ozhiitaa *vai* s/he gets ready, prepares
ozhiitaa' *vta* get him/her ready, prepare him/her
ozhitoon *vti2* make it, build it
-sago *pc disc* (discourse particle cluster: **isa go**)
wanendan *vti* forget it
wanii'igaans, -an *ni* little trap
wanii'ige *vai* s/he traps
wanitoon *vti* lose it
wawiyazh *adv man* funny
Wayaabishkiiwejig *na-v* white people
wayeshkad *adv tmp* at first, in the beginning
waabam *vta* see him/her
waaban *vii* it is dawn
waabanda' *vta* show it to him/her
waabandan *vti* see it
waabang *vii* tomorrow (conjunct form of **waaban**)
waabishkizi *vai* s/he is white in color

123

waabooz, -oog *na* rabbit
waagaakwad, -oon *ni* ax
waakaa'igan, -an *ni* house, building
waanikaan, -an *ni* a hole that's been dug
waanike *vai* s/he digs a hole
waasechigan, -an *ni* window
Waashtanong *name place* Washington, D.C.
waawaashkeshiwayaan, -ag *na* deer hide
waawanoons, -an *ni* little egg
waazakonenjigan, -an *ni* light
wegwaagi *pc disc* behold
wenda- *pv lex* really (see also **enda-**)
wenipanendan *vti* consider it to be easy
wenji- *pv rel* from where, why (changed form of **onji-**)
weshki-bimaadizijig *na-v* young people
wiidookaazo *vai* s/he helps
wiigiwaam, -an *ni* wigwam, lodge
wiigwaas, -an *ni* birch bark
wiigwaasi-jiimaan, -an *ni* birch bark canoe
wiigwaasi-makak, -oon *ni* birch bark box, container
wiiji' *vta* play with him/her
wiijiiw *vta* accompany him/her, go with him/her
wiijiiwaagan, -ag *na* companion, partner
wiikobizh /wiikobiN-/ *vta* pull him/her
wiikwajitoon *vti* try to do it
wiindamaw *vta* tell him/her
wiinizisimaan, -an *ni* wig (also **owiinizisimaan**)
wiisini *vai* s/he eats
wiisiniwin *ni* food
wiiyaas *ni* meat
wiiyaw *nid* his/her body
zagaskwaajime, -g *na* leech
zagaswaa *vai* s/he smokes

zagaswaazh /zagaswaaN-/ *vta* smoke him/her
zagaswe'idi- *vai* have a ceremony
zaziikizi *vai* s/he is the eldest sibling
zaaga'igan, -iin *ni* lake
zaagibagaa *vii* leaves bud
zaagijiwebin *vta* throw him/her outside
zaagitoon *vti* treasure it, be stingy with it
zaasakokwaan, -ag *na* fry bread
zegi' *vta* scare him/her
zegizi *vai* s/he is scared
zeziikizijig *na-v* the oldest children (see also **zaziikizi**)
Zhaaganaashii-aki *name place* Canada (also **Zhaaganaashiiwaki**)
zhaaganaashiimo *vai* s/he speaks English
zhaangweshi, -wag *na* mink
zhizhoobii' /zhizhoobii'W-/ *vta* paint him/her
zhizhoobii'odizo *vai* s/he paints herself/himself
zhiiwaagamizigan *ni* syrup
zhooniyaake *vai* s/he makes money, earns money
ziiga'igaans, -an *ni* little sugar cake
ziigigamide *vii* it boils over
ziigwan *vii* it is spring
ziigwebinan *vti* spill it
ziigwebinigaade *vii* it is spilled, it is dumped out, they dump it out
ziinzibaakwad *ni* maple sugar
ziinzibaakwadoons *ni* maple sugar, candy

Dorothy Dora Whipple, Mezinaashiikwe, is an elder from the Leech Lake Reservation in Minnesota. She has spoken Ojibwe her entire life and has worked on numerous Ojibwe language revitalization projects, including the University of Minnesota's Ojibwe Language CD-ROM Project. She made audio recordings for and helped to design all five of the CDs that project produced: *Manoominikewin: Wild Ricing, Asemaa: Tobacco, Wanii'igewin miinawaa Agoodoowin: Trapping and Snaring, Izhi-ningo-biboon: One Whole Year,* and *Endaayang: Our House.* She now lives in Minneapolis.

Wendy Makoons Geniusz is assistant professor in the Department of Languages at the University of Wisconsin–Eau Claire, where she teaches the Ojibwe language. She is author of *Our Knowledge Is Not Primitive: Decolonizing Botanical Anishinaabe Teachings* and editor of *Plants Have So Much to Give Us, All We Have to Do Is Ask: Anishinaabe Botanical Teachings* by Mary Siisip Geniusz (Minnesota, 2015).

Brendan Fairbanks is assistant professor of American Indian studies at the University of Minnesota. As a linguist and language activist, he is involved in the documentation and preservation of the Ojibwe language.

Also Published by the University of Minnesota Press

The Mishomis Book: The Voice of the Ojibway

Edward Benton-Banai

Portage Lake: Memories of an Ojibwe Childhood

Maude Kegg

Plants Have So Much to Give Us, All We Have to Do Is Ask: Anishinaabe Botanical Teachings

Mary Siisip Geniusz

A Concise Dictionary of Minnesota Ojibwe

John D. Nichols and Earl Nyholm

Indians in Minnesota

Kathy Davis Graves and Elizabeth Ebbott

Survival Schools: The American Indian Movement and Community Education in the Twin Cities

Julie L. Davis